WHY THE INNOCENT PLEAD GUILTY AND THE GUILTY GO FREE

JED S. RAKOFF

FARRAR, STRAUS AND GIROUX ■ NEW YORK

WHY
THE INNOCENT
PLEAD GUILTY
AND
THE GUILTY
GO FREE

AND OTHER
PARADOXES OF
OUR BROKEN
LEGAL SYSTEM

Farrar, Straus and Giroux
120 Broadway, New York, 10271

Library of Congress Cataloging-in-Publication Data
Names: Rakoff, Jed S., author.
Title: Why the innocent plead guilty and the guilty go free : and other
    paradoxes of our broken legal system / Jed S. Rakoff.
Description: First edition. | New York : Farrar, Straus and Giroux, 2021.
    Includes index. | Summary: "A senior federal judge's incisive, unsettling
    exploration of some of the paradoxes that define the judiciary today: among
    them, why innocent people plead guilty, why high-level executives aren't
    prosecuted, why you won't get your day in court, and why the judiciary
    is curtailing its own constitutionally mandated power" —Provided by
    publisher.
Identifiers: LCCN 2020043848 | ISBN 9780374289997 (hardcover)
Subjects: LCSH: Judicial error—United States. | False imprisonment—United
    States. | False testimony—United States. | Criminal justice, Administration
    of—United States.
Classification: LCC KF9756 .R35 2021 | DDC 345.73/0122—dc23
LC record available at https://lccn.loc.gov/2020043848

Designed by Abby Kagan

www.fsgbooks.com
www.twitter.com/fsgbooks • www.facebook.com/fsgbooks

To the memory of
Robert B. Silvers
(1929–2017)

CONTENTS

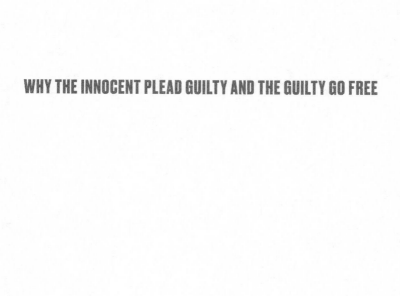

WHY THE INNOCENT PLEAD GUILTY AND THE GUILTY GO FREE

INTRODUCTION

A sense of justice is central to human endurance. No matter what wrongs we suffer or misfortunes we withstand, the belief that justice will ultimately prevail is part of what keeps us going. Nowhere is this belief more deeply felt than in the United States, and with good reason, for over the decades we have made progress, however haltingly and imperfectly, in dealing with poverty, racism, sexism, homophobia, and many other challenges.

But at present our system of justice is facing more than one challenge that it seems unable to come to grips with, perhaps because our faith in it may blind us to its shortcomings and contradictions. How can we be fully proud of a system that locks up more human beings than are imprisoned in any other nation? How can we have confidence in a system that too frequently convicts innocent people—often on the basis of dubious forensic science and shaky eyewitness testimony—and sometimes even coerces them into pleading guilty to crimes they never committed? How can we accept a system that imposes the death penalty when we know full well that a meaningful number of those sentenced to death will later be proved innocent? How can we pretend we are adhering to the Constitution when we have created a criminal justice system in which the jury trial has all but been eliminated? How can we claim that justice is equal when we imprison thousands of poor Black men for relatively modest crimes but almost never prosecute rich, white, high-level executives who commit crimes having far greater impact?

How can we justify using the convenient excuse of the never-ending "war on terror" to narrow rights guaranteed by the Constitution? How can we accept Congress's and the Supreme Court's limiting to the point of near extinction the hallowed constitutional right to habeas corpus relief? How can we applaud the Supreme Court's view of its ever-more-confined role in combating excess by the president?

Finally, how can we tout our system of civil justice as a remedy for wrongs when the great majority of Americans cannot afford to go to court at all, and are often kept out of court even when they wish to avail themselves of its benefits? In these and other important ways, our system of justice is failing its mission.

That our current system of justice is beset by hypocritical pretensions, conundrums, paradoxes, and shortcomings is not a realization I came to easily. When, after serving as a federal prosecutor and then a criminal defense lawyer, I first became a federal judge a quarter century ago, I still thought the system pretty much delivered justice as it was supposed to and just needed some tweaking here and there to get it right. But my subsequent experience and that of my judicial colleagues too often revealed that our system of justice was seriously flawed, and after a while I thought it my duty to speak out about these deficiencies. I tried to do this, first and foremost, in the actual cases that came before me; but over time, recurring patterns emerged in those cases that made me believe I had an obligation to bring these shortcomings to public attention as well.

About six years ago, I began to write articles calling attention to these problems for *The New York Review of Books* (to whose editors I owe a huge debt). This book (which was completed in the summer of 2020) further develops the themes of those articles and also addresses additional limitations of our legal system that have become evident to me from the work I have done on various committees of the National Academy of Sciences, the MacArthur Foundation, and the National Commission on Forensic Science. Finally, the book offers some specific suggestions on how to deal with these problems; but it also argues that real reform must come from an increased recognition by everyday people that our system of justice is broken and needs to be fixed.

1

THE SCOURGE OF MASS INCARCERATION

For too long, too many judges have been too quiet about an evil of which we are a part: the mass incarceration of people in the United States. It is time for more of us to speak out.

The basic facts are not in dispute. As of 2019, more than 2.2 million people were incarcerated in U.S. jails and prisons, a 500 percent increase over the past forty years. Although the United States accounts for about 5 percent of the world's population, it houses nearly 25 percent of the world's prison population. The per capita incarceration rate in the United States is about one and a half times that of second-place El Salvador and third-place Turkmenistan, and more than six times the rate of neighboring Canada. Another 4.75 million Americans are subject to state supervision imposed by probation or parole.

Much of the increase in imprisonment has been for nonviolent offenses, ranging from drug possession to property theft. And even though crime rates in the United States have mostly declined since the early 1990s, the number of incarcerated persons has either risen or remained at levels above 2 million, partly because more people are being sent to prison for offenses that once were punished with other measures, but also because the sentences are longer. For example, even though the number of violent crimes has materially decreased over the past two decades, the number of prisoners serving life sentences has steadily increased, so that one in nine persons in prison is now serving a life sentence. In addition, at least 500,000 of the 2.2 million persons now incarcerated have not been convicted of any crime but are simply there because, having been arrested, they could not make bail.

And whom are we locking up? Mostly young men of color. Over 840,000, or nearly 40 percent, of the 2.2 million U.S. prisoners are African American males. Put another way, about one in nine African American males between the ages of twenty and thirty-four is now in prison, with at least an equal number subject to probationary supervision. If current rates hold, one-third of all Black men will be imprisoned at some point in their lifetimes. Another approximately 440,000, or 20 percent, of the 2.2 million U.S. prisoners are young Hispanic males.

This mass incarceration, which also includes about 800,000 white and Asian males, as well as over 100,000 women (most of whom committed nonviolent offenses), is the product of statutes that were enacted, beginning in the 1970s, with the twin purposes of lowering crime rates in general and deterring the drug trade in particular. These laws imposed mandatory minimum terms of imprisonment on many first offenders. They denied bail to many persons arrested on minor charges that were eventually dropped. They propounded sentencing guidelines that initially mandated, and still recommend, very substantial prison terms for many, if not most, offenders. And they required lifetime imprisonment for many recidivists. These laws also substantially deprived judges of sentencing discretion and effectively guaranteed imprisonment for many offenders who would have previously received probation or deferred prosecution, or who would have been sent to drug treatment or mental health programs rather than prison.

The unavoidable question is whether these laws have succeeded in reducing crime. Certainly crime rates have come down substantially from the very high levels of the 1970s and 1980s. Overall, crime rates have been cut nearly in half since they reached their peak in 1991, and, even taking into account the unusual spike in shootings in some cities that accompanied the stresses of the COVID-19 pandemic, crime rates in general are now at levels not seen in many decades. A simple but powerful argument can be made that, by locking up for extended periods the people who are most likely to commit crimes, we have both incapacitated those who would otherwise be recidivists and deterred still others from committing crimes in the first place.

But is this true? The honest answer is that we don't know. And it is this uncertainty that makes changing the status quo so difficult: Why tamper, the argument goes, with what seems to be working unless we know that it isn't working?

There are some who claim that they do know whether our increased rate of incarceration is the primary cause of the decline in crime. These are the sociologists, the economists, the statisticians, and others who assert that they have "scientifically" determined the answer. But their answers are all over the place. Thus, for example, a 2002 study by the sociologist Thomas Arvanites and the economist Robert DeFina claimed that, while increased incarceration accounted for 21 percent of the large decline in property crime during the 1990s, it had no effect on the similarly large decline in violent crime. But two years later, in 2004, the economist Steven Levitt—of *Freakonomics* fame—claimed that incarceration accounted for no less than 32 percent of the decline in crime during that period.

Levitt's conclusions, in turn, were questioned in 2006, when the sociologist Bruce Western reexamined the data and claimed that only about 10 percent of the crime drop in the 1990s could be attributed to increased incarceration. But two years after that, in 2008, the criminologist Eric Baumer took still another look at the same data and found that they could support claims that increased incarceration accounted for anywhere between 10 and 35 percent of the decrease in crime in the 1990s.

As these examples illustrate, there is nothing close to an academic consensus on the proportion of the decrease in crime attributable to increased incarceration. In 2014, a distinguished committee of the National Research Council of the National Academy of Sciences, after reviewing the studies I have mentioned as well as a great many more, was able to conclude only that while most of the studies "support the conclusion that the growth in incarceration rates reduced crime . . . the magnitude of the crime reduction remains highly uncertain."

To illustrate the difficulties, consider a study titled "What Caused the Crime Decline?"—published in February 2015 by the Brennan Center for Justice at NYU Law School—which purports to show that increased incarceration has been responsible for only a negligible decrease in crime. One cannot help but be impressed by the sheer scope of the study. The authors identify the fourteen most popular theories for the decline in crime in the last few decades and attempt to test each of them against the available data.

Five of the theories involve criminal justice policies: increased incarceration, increased numbers of police and prosecutors, increased use of statistics in devising police strategies to combat crime, threat of the death penalty, and enactment of right-to-carry gun laws (which theoretically deter violent criminals because potential victims might be armed). Another four of the theories involve economics: changes in unemployment, income, inflation, and consumer confidence. The final five theories involve environmental and social factors: aging population, decreased alcohol consumption, decreased crack use, legalized abortion, and decreased lead in gasoline (which theoretically reduces the supposed tendency of lead fumes to cause overaggressive behavior).

The primary findings of the Brennan Center study are that "increased incarceration has had little effect on the drop in violent crime in the past 24 years" and has "accounted for less than 1 percent of the decline in property crime this century." To reach these striking results, the authors rely (as did most of the earlier studies cited above) on the social scientist's favorite method, a multivariable regression analysis that "controls for the effects of each variable on crime, and each variable on other variables." But as anyone familiar with regression analysis knows, it rarely speaks to causality, as opposed to correlation; and even to show correlation, the analysis involves a lot of educated guesswork. The authors admit as much, but they seek to downplay the level of uncertainty, stating: "There is always some uncertainty and statistical error involved in any empirical analysis." But when you are dealing with matters as difficult to measure as how much of the decrease in crime can be attributed to everything from decreased alcohol consumption to increased consumer confidence, your so-called estimates may be little more than speculations.

In an attempt to adjust to this difficulty, the authors state the percentage of crime decrease attributable to each given factor as a range. For example, increased police numbers accounted, according to the study, for 0 to 5 percent of the decline in crime between 1990 and 2013. But if you take the low end of each of the ranges, the fourteen factors analyzed in the Brennan Center study collectively accounted for as little as 10 percent of the decline in crime over that period; and even if you take the high end of each of the ranges, the various factors still accounted for only 40 percent of the decline in crime. Under any analysis, therefore, either the decline in crime in the last twenty-five years or so was chiefly the product of forces that none of the leading theorists has identified, or (as seems more likely) the regression analysis used by the authors of the Brennan Center study is too imperfect a tool to be of much use in this kind of situation.

My point is not to criticize the Brennan Center study. It is in many respects the most ambitious and comprehensive study of its kind undertaken to date. But as the National Research Council report points out in discussing the many similar studies that, as noted, led to a wide range of results, there are simply too many variables, uncertainties, estimates, and challenges involved in the question to rely on a regression analysis that is little more than speculation dressed up as statistics. The result is that one cannot fairly claim to know with any degree of confidence or precision the relative role of increased incarceration in decreasing crime.

Put another way, the supposition on which our mass incarceration is premised—namely, that it materially reduces crime—is, at best, a hunch. Yet the price we pay for acting on this hunch is enormous. This is true in the literal sense: it costs more than $180 billion a year to run our jails and prisons. It is also true in the social sense: by locking up so many young men, most of them men of color, we contribute to the erosion of family and community life in ways that harm generations of children, while creating a future cadre of disenfranchised, unemployable ex-convicts, many of whom have learned in prison how better to commit future crimes. And it is even true in the symbolic sense: by locking up, sooner or later, one out of every three African American males, we send a message that our society has no better cure for racial disparities than brute force.

So why do we have mass incarceration? More than anything, it is because the laws that were passed in response to the substantial rise in crime rates in the thirty years between 1960 and 1990 remain politically popular. These laws varied widely in their specifics, but they had two common characteristics: they imposed higher penalties, and they removed much of judicial discretion in sentencing.

The most pernicious of these laws were the statutes imposing mandatory minimum terms of imprisonment. Although there were a few such laws prior to 1970, thereafter Congress passed numerous laws dictating relatively harsh mandatory minimum terms of imprisonment for a very wide variety of criminal violations. Most notably, these laws imposed mandatory minimums of five, ten, and twenty years for various drug offenses, and as much as twenty-five additional years for possession of guns during drug trafficking. But they also imposed mandatory minimum terms of imprisonment for such widely varying offenses as possession of child pornography, aggravated identity theft, transportation of aliens into the United States for commercial advantage, hostage taking, unlawful possession of antiaircraft missiles, assault on U.S. service members, stalking other persons in violation of a restraining order, and fraudulent use of food stamp access devices. The dictate common to all these laws was that, no matter how minor the offender's participation in the offense may have been, and no matter what mitigating circumstances might have been present, the judge was required to send the offender to prison, often for a substantial number of years. So, for example, a courier who, in return for a few hundred dollars, delivered a small quantity of drugs to one or two customers might still face a mandatory minimum prison sentence of five years, ten years, or even more if she was part of a loosely connected ring that collectively distributed a large quantity of the drugs.

Throughout the 1970s and 1980s, many of the fifty states—with the full support of the federal government, which hugely increased its funding for state prisons during these years—passed similar mandatory minimum laws, and some went a step further and imposed mandatory minimum sentences of life imprisonment for recidivists (California's "three strikes" law being a noteworthy example). Not to be outdone, Congress not only passed "career offender" laws similar to the "three strikes" statute but also, in 1984, enacted, with bipartisan support, the federal sentencing guidelines. These guidelines, although initially intended to minimize disparities in sentencing, quickly became a vehicle for greatly increased sentences for virtually every federal crime, chiefly because Congress repeatedly instructed the Sentencing Commission to raise their levels.

Moreover, these so-called guidelines were, for their first twenty-one years, mandatory and binding. And while, in 2005, the Supreme Court declared that they were unconstitutional unless discretionary, federal judges are still required to treat them as the starting point for determining any sentence, with the result that they continue to be followed in most cases. More generally, both state and federal judges became accustomed to imposing prison terms as the norm; and with the passage of time, there were fewer and fewer judges on the bench who had ever experienced a gentler approach.

But why, given the great decline in crime in the last quarter century, have most of the draconian laws that created these harsh norms not been repealed or at least moderated? Some observers, like Michelle Alexander in her influential book *The New Jim Crow* (2010), assert that it is a case of thinly disguised racism. Others, mostly of an economic determinist persuasion, claim that it is the result of the rise of a powerful private prison industry that has an economic stake in continuing mass incarceration.

Still others blame everything from a continuing reaction to the "excesses" of the 1960s to the never-ending nature of the "war on drugs" to the sheer increase in the number of both police officers and prosecutors, who view it as their role to ensure public safety by sending more and more people to prison.

While there may be something to each of these theories, a simpler explanation is that most Americans, having noticed that the crime-ridden environment of the 1970s and 1980s was replaced by the much safer environment of today only after tough sentencing laws went into force, are reluctant to tamper with the laws they believe made them safer. They are not impressed with academic studies that question this belief, suspecting that the authors have their own axes to grind; and they are repelled by those who question their good faith, since they perceive nothing racist in wanting a crime-free environment. Ironically, the one thing that might convince them that mass incarceration is not the solution to their safety would be if crime rates continued to decrease when incarceration rates were reduced. But although this has in fact happened in a few places, people in most communities are not willing to take the chance of such an experiment, and occasional new spikes in one crime or another reinforce that rigidity.

This, then, is a classic case of members of the public relying on what they believe is common sense and being resentful of those who question their motives and dispute their intelligence. What is called for in such circumstances is leadership: those whom the public does respect should point out why statutes prescribing mandatory minimums, draconian guidelines, and the like are not the solution to controlling crime, and why, in any case, the long-term price of mass incarceration is too high to pay, not just in economic terms but also in terms of wasted lives, devastated families, and racial bias.

Until quite recently, that leadership appeared to be missing in both the legislative and executive branches, since being labeled soft on crime was politically dangerous. In late 2018, however, Congress passed, and the president signed, the aptly named First Step Act, which retroactively reduces mandatory minimum terms of incarceration for nonviolent drug offenses. This has already led, in my court as elsewhere, to substantial reductions in sentences for nonviolent offenders, who were often serving mandatory terms of thirty years and more. But, as the name indicates, this is but a first step in reducing mass incarceration, and has in fact reduced incarceration totals by only a small amount. It does not begin to eliminate federal mandatory minimums altogether. It does not address the situation in the state courts, where most mass incarceration occurs. It does nothing to address the common tendency of both state and federal prosecutors to charge suspects with the most serious offenses available, thereby greatly increasing the likelihood of prison time. And most fundamentally, it does nothing to erase the now ingrained assumption that a prison term is the "natural" and best response to social misconduct.

So where in all this stands the judiciary? In some ways, this should be our issue, not just because sentencing has historically been the prerogative of judges but also because it is we judges who are forced to impose sentences that many of us feel are unjust and counterproductive. It is probably too much to ask state judges in the thirty-seven states where judges are elected to adopt a position that could be characterized as "soft on crime." But what about the federal judiciary, which is protected by lifetime tenure from political retaliation and, according to most polls, is generally well regarded by the public as a whole?

On one issue—mandatory minimum laws—the federal judiciary has been consistent in its opposition and clear in its message. As stated in a September 2013 letter to Congress submitted by the Judicial Conference of the United States (the governing board of federal judges), "For sixty years, the Judicial Conference has consistently and vigorously opposed mandatory minimum sentences and has supported measures for their repeal or to ameliorate their effects." But nowhere in the nine single-spaced pages that follow is any reference made to the evils of mass incarceration; indeed, most federal judges continue to support the prison-favoring federal sentencing guidelines, which, while no longer mandatory, still provide the basis on which most federal sentences are formulated. As for Congress, while occasionally approving reductions in the guidelines recommended by the Sentencing Commission, it has much more often required the Sentencing Commission to increase the prison time reflected in those guidelines, thereby further supporting mass incarceration.

Yet even within the judiciary there is some modest cause for hope. Several brave federal district judges—such as Lynn Adelman of Wisconsin, Mark Bennett of Iowa, Paul Friedman of the District of Columbia, and Michael Ponsor of Massachusetts, as well as former federal judges Paul Cassell and Nancy Gertner—have for some time openly denounced the policy of mass incarceration. More recently, a federal appellate judge, Gerard Lynch of New York, wrote: "The United States has a vastly overinflated system of incarceration that is excessively punitive, disproportionate in its impact on the poor and minorities, exceedingly expensive, and largely irrelevant to reducing predatory crime."

In many respects, the people of the United States can be proud of the progress we have made over the past half century in promoting racial equality. More haltingly, we have also made some progress in our treatment of the poor and disadvantaged. But the big, glaring exception to both these improvements is how we treat those guilty of crimes. Basically, we treat them like dirt. And while this treatment is mandated by the legislature, it is we judges who mete it out. Unless we judges make more effort to speak out against this inhumanity, how can we call ourselves instruments of justice?

2

WHY INNOCENT PEOPLE PLEAD GUILTY

The criminal justice system in the United States today bears little relationship to what the Founding Fathers contemplated, what the media portray, or what the average American believes.

To the Founding Fathers, the critical element in the system was the jury trial, which served not only as a truth-seeking mechanism and a means of achieving fairness but also as a shield against tyranny. As Thomas Jefferson famously said, "I consider [trial by jury] as the only anchor ever yet imagined by man, by which a government can be held to the principles of its constitution."

The Sixth Amendment to the U.S. Constitution guarantees that "in all criminal prosecutions, the accused shall enjoy the right to a speedy and public trial, by an impartial jury." The Constitution further guarantees that at the trial, the accused will have the assistance of counsel, who can confront and cross-examine his accusers and present evidence on the accused's behalf. The accused may be convicted only if an impartial jury of his peers is unanimously of the view that he is guilty beyond a reasonable doubt and so states, publicly, in its verdict.

The drama inherent in these guarantees is regularly portrayed in movies and television programs as an open battle played out in public before a judge and jury. But this is all a mirage. In actuality, our criminal justice system is almost exclusively a system of plea bargaining, negotiated behind closed doors and with no judicial oversight. The outcome is very largely determined by the prosecutor alone. ·

In 2018, while 8 percent of all federal criminal charges were dismissed (either because of a mistake in fact or law or because the defendant had decided to cooperate), more than 97 percent of the remainder were resolved through plea bargains, and fewer than 3 percent went to trial. This figure has been consistent for the last twenty years or more. The plea bargains, in turn, largely determine the sentences imposed.

While corresponding statistics for the fifty states combined are not fully available, it is a rare state where plea bargains do not similarly account for the resolution of at least 95 percent of the felony cases that are not dismissed; and again, the plea bargains usually determine the sentences, either as a matter of law (because the sentence is mandatory) or as a matter of practice (because judges tend to follow the parties' jointly stipulated sentencing guideline range and the like). Furthermore, in both the state and federal systems, the power to determine the terms of the plea bargain is, as a practical matter, lodged largely in the prosecutor, with the defense counsel having little negotiating power.

It was not always so. Until roughly the end of the Civil War, plea bargains were exceedingly rare. A criminal defendant would either go to trial or simply confess and plead guilty to the charge laid against him. If the defendant was convicted, the judge would have wide discretion in determining the sentence; and that decision, made with little input from the parties, was subject only to the most modest appellate review.

After the Civil War, this began to change, chiefly because, as a result of the disruptions and dislocations that followed the war, as well as the stresses (economic and otherwise) accompanying greatly increased immigration, crime rates rose considerably, and a way had to be found to dispose of cases without imposing an impossible burden on the criminal justice system. Plea bargains offered a way out: by pleading guilty to lesser charges in return for dismissal of the more serious charges, defendants could reduce their prison time, while the prosecution could resolve the case without burdening the system with more trials.

The practice of plea bargaining never really took hold in most other countries, where it was viewed as a kind of devil's pact that allowed guilty defendants to avoid the full force of the law. But in the United States it became commonplace. And while the Supreme Court initially expressed reservations about the system of plea bargaining, eventually the Court came to approve of it as an exercise in contractual negotiation between independent agents (the prosecutor and the defense counsel) that was helpful in making the system work.

Plea bargains eventually came to account, in the years immediately following World War II, for the resolution of over 80 percent of all criminal cases (state and federal) that were not dismissed. But even then, perhaps, there were enough cases still going to trial, and enough power remaining with defense counsel, to keep the system honest. By this I mean that a genuinely innocent defendant could still choose to go to trial without fearing that, if she was somehow convicted, she might thereby subject herself to an extremely long prison term effectively dictated by the prosecutor. And the prosecutor had to contemplate the possibility that a meaningful number of cases would still go to trial, and so had to be careful not to engage in any practices that would be harmful or embarrassing in the eyes of a jury, a judge, or the community at large if a public trial did occur.

All this changed in the 1970s and 1980s, and, as with mass incarceration (see chapter 1), it was once again in reaction to rising crime rates. While the 1950s were a period of relatively low crime rates in the United States, rates began to rise substantially in the 1960s, and by 1980 or so, serious crime, much of it drug-related, was occurring at a frequency not seen for many decades. As a result, state and federal legislatures hugely increased the penalties for criminal violations. In New York, for example, the so-called Rockefeller Laws, enacted in 1973, dictated a minimum sentence of fifteen years' imprisonment for selling just two ounces (or possessing four ounces) of heroin, cocaine, or marijuana. In addition, in response to what was perceived as a tendency of too many judges to impose too lenient sentences, the new, enhanced sentences were frequently made mandatory and, in those thirty-seven states where judges were elected, many "soft" judges were defeated and "tough on crime" judges elected in their place.

At the federal level, Congress imposed mandatory minimum sentences for narcotics offenses, gun offenses, child pornography offenses, and (as discussed in chapter 1) much else besides. Sometimes, moreover, these mandatory sentences were required to be imposed consecutively. For example, federal law prescribes a mandatory minimum of ten years' imprisonment, and a maximum of life imprisonment, for participating in a conspiracy that distributes five kilograms or more of cocaine. But if the use of a weapon is involved, the defendant, even if she had a low-level role in the conspiracy, must be sentenced to a mandatory minimum of fifteen years' imprisonment (i.e., ten years on the drug count and five years on the weapons count). And if two weapons are involved, the mandatory minimum rises to forty years (i.e., ten years on the drug count, five years on the first weapons count, and twenty-five years on the second weapons count)—all of these sentences being mandatory, with the judge having no power to reduce them.

In addition to mandatory minimums, Congress in 1984 introduced—with bipartisan support—a regime of mandatory sentencing guidelines designed to avoid "irrational" sentencing disparities. Since these guidelines were not as draconian as the mandatory minimum sentences, and since they left judges with some limited discretion, it was not perceived at first how, perhaps even more than mandatory minimums, such a guidelines regime (which was enacted in many states as well) transferred power over sentencing away from judges and into the hands of prosecutors.

One thing that did become quickly apparent, however, was that these guidelines, along with mandatory minimums, were causing the virtual extinction of jury trials in federal criminal cases. Thus, whereas in 1980, 19 percent of all federal defendants went to trial, by 2000 the number had decreased to less than 6 percent and by 2010 to less than 3 percent, where it has remained ever since. In the states, the figure for criminal cases going to trial is now almost down to 2 percent.

The reason for this is that the guidelines, like the mandatory minimums, provide prosecutors with weapons to bludgeon defendants into effectively coerced plea bargains. In the majority of criminal cases, a defense lawyer meets her client only when or shortly after the client is arrested, so that, at the outset, she is at a considerable informational disadvantage to the prosecutor. If, as is very often the case (despite the constitutional prohibition of "excessive bail" and so-called "bail reform" in a few localities), bail is set so high that the client is detained, the defense lawyer has only modest opportunities, within the limited visiting hours and other arduous restrictions imposed by most jails, to interview her client and find out his version of the facts.

The prosecutor, by contrast, will typically have a full police report, complete with witness interviews and other evidence, shortly followed by grand jury testimony, forensic test reports, and follow-up investigations. While (as discussed in chapters 3 and 5) much of this may be one-sided and inaccurate, it not only gives the prosecutor a huge advantage over the defense counsel but also makes the prosecutor confident, maybe overconfident, in the strength of his case.

Against this background, the information-deprived defense lawyer, typically within a few days after the arrest, meets with the overconfident prosecutor, who makes clear that, unless the case can be promptly resolved by a plea bargain, he intends to charge the defendant with the most severe offenses he can prove. Indeed, for several decades now, prosecutors in many jurisdictions have been required by their superiors to charge the defendant with the most serious charges that can be proved—unless, of course, the defendant is willing to enter into a plea bargain. If the defendant wants to plead guilty, the prosecutor will offer him a considerably reduced charge—but only if the plea is agreed to promptly (thus saving the prosecutor valuable resources). Otherwise, he will charge the maximum, and, while he will not close the door to any later plea bargain, it will be to a higher-level offense than the one offered at the outset of the case.

In this typical situation, the prosecutor has all the advantages. He knows a lot about the case (and, as noted, probably feels more confident about it than he should, since he has only heard from one side), whereas the defense lawyer knows very little. Furthermore, notwithstanding the nominal requirement that criminal charges be presented to a grand jury, in actuality the prosecutor effectively controls the decision to charge the defendant with whatever crimes he chooses. Indeed, the law of every U.S. jurisdiction leaves the drafting of criminal indictments to the prosecutor's unfettered discretion; and both the prosecutor and the defense lawyer know that the grand jury, which typically will hear from one side only, is highly likely to approve any charge the prosecutor recommends.

But what really puts the prosecutor in the driver's seat is the fact that the prosecutor—because of mandatory minimums, sentencing guidelines, and simply his ability to shape whatever charges are brought—can effectively dictate the sentence by how he drafts the indictment. For example, the prosecutor can agree with the defense counsel in a federal narcotics case that, if there is a plea bargain, the defendant will have to plead guilty only to the personal sale of a few ounces of heroin, which carries no mandatory minimum and a guidelines range of less than two years; but if the defendant does not plead guilty, he will be charged with the drug conspiracy of which his sale was a small part, a conspiracy involving many kilograms of heroin, which could mean a ten-year mandatory minimum and a guidelines range of twenty years or more. Put another way, it is the prosecutor, not the judge, who effectively exercises the sentencing power, albeit cloaked as a charging decision.

The defense lawyer understands this fully, and so she recognizes that the best outcome for her client is likely to be an early plea bargain, while the prosecutor is still willing to accept a plea to a relatively low-level offense. Indeed, in the past decade, the average prison sentence for federal narcotics defendants who entered into plea bargains has been around five years, while the average sentence for those few federal narcotics defendants who exercised their right to trial but were found guilty has been in excess of fifteen years—an average "trial penalty" of ten years in prison.

Although under pressure to agree to the first plea bargain offered, prudent defense counsel will try to convince the prosecutor to give her some time to explore legal and factual defenses; but the prosecutor, often overworked and understaffed, may not agree. Defense counsel, moreover, is in no position to abruptly refuse the prosecutor's proposal, since, under recent Supreme Court decisions, she will face a claim of "ineffective assistance of counsel" if, without consulting her client, she summarily rejects a proposed plea bargain.

Defense counsel also recognizes that, even if she thinks the plea bargain being offered is unfair compared to those offered by other, similarly situated prosecutors, she has little or no recourse. An appeal to the prosecutor's superior will rarely succeed, since the superiors feel the need to support their troops and since, once again, the prosecutor can shape the facts so as to make his superior find his proposed plea acceptable. And there is no way defense counsel can appeal to a neutral third party, the judge, since in all but a few jurisdictions, the judiciary is precluded from participating in plea-bargain negotiations. In a word, she and her client are stuck.

Though there are many variations on this theme, they all prove the same basic point: the prosecutor has all the power. The Supreme Court's suggestion that a plea bargain is a fair and voluntary contractual arrangement between two relatively equal parties is a total myth: it is much more like a "contract of adhesion" in which one party can effectively force its will on the other party.

The result is that, of the 2.2 million Americans now in jail or prison—an appalling number in its own right—over 1.6 million (i.e., those in prison versus jail) are there as a result of plea bargains dictated by the government's prosecutors, who effectively dictate the sentences as well. And most of the remaining 0.6 million or so (i.e., those in jail versus prison), while nominally awaiting trial, are really just waiting for word of what plea bargains the prosecutor will accept.

A cynic might ask: What's wrong with that? After all, crime rates have declined over the past twenty-plus years to levels not seen since the early 1960s, and while, as suggested in chapter 1, there are many theories as to why this has occurred, it may not be unreasonable to assume that the enhanced penalties described above, by giving prosecutors the power to force criminals to accept significant jail terms, has played a material part in this reduction. Most Americans feel a lot safer today than they did just a few decades ago, and that feeling has contributed substantially to their enjoyment of life. Why should we cavil at the empowering of prosecutors that has brought us this result?

The answer may be found in Jefferson's insight that a criminal justice system that is secret and government-dictated ultimately invites abuse and even tyranny. More specifically, the current system of prosecutor-determined plea bargaining suffers from some severe infirmities.

First, it is grossly one-sided and inconsistent with our constitutional and institutional notions of fair play. Our criminal justice system, as embodied in the federal Constitution and the constitutions of all fifty states, is premised on the notion that, before we deprive a person of his liberty, he will have his day in court. He will have a trial by his peers, at which he will be able to put the government to its proof and present his own facts and arguments. He will not be deprived of his liberty unless the jury has unanimously found that he is guilty beyond a reasonable doubt. And, even then, he will not be sent to prison until a neutral judge determines that such punishment is warranted. While we still pay lip service to these guarantees, in actuality the current system of plea-bargained justice contains none of these protections in any real sense.

Second, the current plea-bargaining system is largely secret and unreviewable, in ways that invite inconsistency at best and oppression at worst. Plea bargains are mostly the product of secret negotiations behind closed doors in the prosecutor's office, and are subject to almost no review, either internally or by the courts. Such a secretive system inevitably invites arbitrary results. Indeed, there is a great irony in the fact that legislative measures that were designed to rectify the perceived evils of disparity and arbitrariness in sentencing have empowered prosecutors to preside over a plea-bargaining system that is so secretive and without rules that we do not even know whether or not it operates in an arbitrary manner.

Third, and possibly the gravest objection of all, the prosecutor-dictated plea-bargain system, by creating such inordinate pressures to enter into plea bargains, appears to have led a significant number of defendants to plead guilty to crimes they never actually committed. For example, of the more than three hundred people whom the Innocence Project and its affiliated lawyers have proved were wrongfully convicted of such serious crimes as rape or murder—crimes that they did not in fact commit—around 10 percent pleaded guilty to those crimes. Some of these innocents pleaded guilty because they were accused of capital crimes and so faced the possibility of the death penalty if they were erroneously convicted. But other innocents pleaded guilty simply because they had no confidence in the likelihood of their exoneration and so sought to cut their losses. And statistics from the National Registry of Exonerations (a joint project of three law schools) suggest that this self-protective psychology is a widespread problem, not just in the very serious cases handled by the Innocence Project but in less serious cases as well. Specifically, the National Registry of Exonerations records that of more than 2,400 defendants who, having previously been convicted of state or federal felonies, were thereafter determined by the courts to be both legally and factually innocent (i.e., exonerated) between 1989 and 2019, about 9 to 10 percent (i.e., well over 200 persons) had pleaded guilty to crimes of which they were totally innocent.

It is not difficult to perceive why this happens. After all, the typical person accused of a crime combines a troubled past with limited resources: he thus recognizes that, even if he is innocent, his chances of mounting an effective defense at trial may be modest at best. His experiences with the criminal justice system may also have made him cynical about its objectivity, particularly if he is a person of color. Thus, if his lawyer can obtain a plea bargain that will reduce his likely time in prison, he may find it "rational" to take the plea.

Every criminal defense lawyer (and I was both a federal prosecutor and a criminal defense lawyer before going on the bench) has had the experience of a client who first tells his lawyer he is innocent and then, when confronted with a preview of the government's proof, says he is guilty. Usually, he is in fact guilty and was previously lying to his lawyer (despite the protections of the attorney–client privilege, which many defendants, suspicious even of their court-appointed lawyers, do not appreciate). But sometimes the situation is reversed, and the client now lies to his lawyer by saying he is guilty when in fact he is not, because he has decided to take the fall.

In theory, this charade should be exposed at the time the defendant enters his plea, since the judge is supposed to question the defendant about the facts underlying his confession of guilt. But in practice, most judges, happy for their own reasons to avoid a time-consuming trial, will hardly question the defendant beyond the bare bones of his assertion of guilt, relying instead on the prosecutor's statement (untested by any cross-examination) of what the underlying facts are. Indeed, in situations in which the prosecutor and defense counsel themselves recognize that the guilty plea is somewhat artificial, they will have jointly arrived at a written statement of guilt for the defendant to read that cleverly covers all the bases without providing much detail. The Supreme Court, for its part, has gone so far (in the *Alford* case of 1970) as to allow a defendant to enter a guilty plea while factually maintaining his innocence, as part of a "voluntary" plea bargain designed to avoid the "risk" of a wrongful conviction at trial. And while "*Alford* pleas" are rare in the federal courts, they are not uncommon in some states.

Although a defendant's decision to plead guilty to a crime he did not commit may represent a rational, if cynical, cost-benefit analysis of his situation, in fact there is some evidence that the pressure of the situation may cause an innocent defendant to make a less-than-rational appraisal of his chances for acquittal and thus decide to plead guilty when he not only is actually innocent but also could be proved so. Research indicates that young, unintelligent, or risk-averse defendants will often provide false confessions just because they cannot take the heat of an interrogation. While research into false guilty pleas is far less developed, it may be hypothesized that similar pressures, less immediate but more prolonged, may be in effect when a defendant, already in jail because he was denied bail, is told, often by his own lawyer, that there is a strong case against him, that his likelihood of acquittal is low, and that he faces a mandatory minimum of five or ten years in prison if convicted and a guidelines range of considerably more—but that, if he acts swiftly, he can get a plea bargain to a lesser offense that will reduce his prison time by many years.

How prevalent is the phenomenon of innocent people pleading guilty? As noted, both the Innocence Project and the National Registry of Exonerations report that 9 to 10 percent of exonerees pleaded guilty to crimes of which they were later shown to be totally innocent. This might, however, overstate the situation, because the cases in which exonerations are pursued are often cases about which there already existed sufficient doubt as to cause reexamination. The few criminologists who have thus far investigated the phenomenon estimate that the overall rate for convicted felons as a whole is between 2 and 8 percent. The size of that range suggests the imperfection of the data; but let us suppose that it is somewhere in between, say 5 percent. When you recall that, of the 2.2 million Americans in jail or prison, most are there either because they have already entered into plea bargains or are in the process of negotiating plea bargains, we are then talking about approximately 100,000 persons or more who are incarcerated for serious crimes to which they have pleaded or are about to plead guilty but did not in fact commit. These innocent people have had their lives effectively destroyed by a system that bears none of the protections in practice that it is supposed to have in theory.

What can we do about it? If there were the political will to do so, we could eliminate mandatory minimums, eliminate sentencing guidelines, and dramatically reduce the severity of our sentencing regimes in general. But as indicated in chapter 1, only a moderate first step has been taken in this direction. It should also be noted that even that first step, which modestly reduced mandatory minimums for certain federal narcotics offenses, encountered stiff opposition. For example, the National Association of Assistant U.S. Attorneys—essentially the alumni association of former federal prosecutors—sent an open letter of opposition, while a similar letter denouncing the bill was signed by two former U.S. attorneys general, three former chiefs of the Drug Enforcement Administration, and eighteen former U.S. attorneys.

More generally, being "tough on crime" is good politics, a leaning that is unlikely to change in the near future. Indeed, the most common criticism of plea bargaining by the general public is that it permits some notorious criminals to "get off too lightly" with "a slap on the wrist." Rarely, however, do people contemplate the possibility that the defendant may be totally innocent of any charge but is being coerced into pleading to a lesser offense because the consequences of going to trial and losing are too severe to take the risk.

But while it therefore seems unlikely that in the immediate future we will implement the kind of legislative solutions that would substantially reduce the likelihood of coerced plea bargains, two helpful proposals could be effected without the need for new legislation.

The first is one that a few jurisdictions, notably Connecticut and Florida, have begun experimenting with: involving judges in the plea-bargaining process. At present, this is forbidden by judicial rule in the federal courts, and with good reason: for a judge to involve herself runs the risk of compromising her objectivity if no plea bargain is reached. For similar reasons, many federal judges (including me) refuse to involve themselves in settlement negotiations in civil cases, even though, unlike the criminal plea-bargain situation, there is no rule forbidding it. But the problem is solved in civil cases by referring the settlement negotiations to magistrates or special masters who do not report the results to the judges who handle the subsequent proceedings. If the federal rule were changed, the same could be done in the criminal plea-bargain situation.

As I envision it, shortly after an indictment is returned (or perhaps even earlier if an arrest has occurred and the defendant is jailed), a magistrate would meet separately with the prosecutor and the defense counsel, in proceedings that would be recorded but placed under seal, and all present would be provided with the particulars regarding the evidence and issues in the case. In certain circumstances, the magistrate might interview witnesses or examine other evidence, again under seal so as not to compromise any party's strategy. The magistrate might even interview the defendant, under an arrangement in which it would not constitute a waiver of the defendant's Fifth Amendment privilege against self-incrimination.

The prosecutor would, in the meantime, be precluded from making any plea-bargain offer (or threat) while the magistrate was studying the case. Once the magistrate was ready, she would then meet separately with both sides and, if appropriate, make a recommendation, such as to dismiss the case (if she thought the proof was weak), to proceed to trial (if she thought there was no reasonable plea bargain available), or to enter into a plea bargain along lines she might suggest. No party would be required to follow the magistrate's suggestions. Their force, if any, would come from the fact that they were being suggested by a neutral third party who, moreover, was a judicial officer that the prosecutors and the defense lawyers would have to appear before in many other cases.

Would a plan structured along these lines wholly eliminate false guilty pleas? Probably not, but it likely would reduce their number and, more generally, lead to better-informed and fairer plea bargains.

My second proposal—which has not yet been tried anywhere in the United States but builds on existing practices in the United Kingdom—would be to require all state and federal prosecutors to spend six months out of every three years serving as criminal defense lawyers for indigent defendants in districts other than their own. The result, I feel sure, would be to make prosecutors more aware of the one-sided nature of the present plea-bargaining process and thereby cause them to modify their more onerous plea-bargaining practices. In the United Kingdom, the practice, for literally centuries, has been that barristers (i.e., professional trial lawyers) serve contemporaneously as prosecutors in some cases and defense counsel in others, causing them to have a balanced view of the process virtually unknown among either prosecutors or defense lawyers in the United States. To be sure, U.S. prosecutors play a larger role in the system than British barristers; for example, they are frequently involved in the investigative stage of criminal cases, a role in the United Kingdom played by solicitors. So, if my proposal were to be put into effect, very careful attention would have to be paid to avoid conflicts of interest. Nevertheless, there is no doubt in my mind that it could be done and that it would result in far more balanced plea bargaining than exists at present.

3

WHY EYEWITNESS TESTIMONY IS SO OFTEN WRONG

One of the reasons even innocent people plead guilty, as discussed in chapter 2, is their fear that, even though innocent, they will be convicted if they go to trial. One might think this fear is exaggerated, since our trial procedure includes so many seeming protections for the wrongly accused, such as the presumption of innocence, the requirement that the government prove guilt beyond a reasonable doubt, the suppression of improperly obtained evidence, the exclusion of hearsay evidence, and the requirement that a jury of twelve persons be unanimous before a defendant can be found guilty. Indeed, this panoply of procedural protections led the great judge Learned Hand to write, in 1923: "Under our criminal procedure the accused has every advantage. . . . Our procedure has always been haunted by the ghost of the innocent man convicted. It is an unreal dream. What we need to fear is the archaic formalism and the watery sentiment that obstructs, delays, and defeats the prosecution of crime."

We now know for a fact that Hand was wrong. As mentioned

in chapter 2, since 1989 more than 2,400 people previously convicted of felonies have been exonerated by the courts (i.e., determined to have been factually innocent of the crimes of which they were convicted). While, as mentioned, approximately 9 to 10 percent of these pleaded guilty to crimes they had never committed, the other 90 percent went to trial and were found guilty, beyond a reasonable doubt, by juries of their peers. Why, then, did Hand, and these juries, get it so wrong? The answer does not lie in our procedures, which, as Hand notes, are highly protective of the accused. The answer, rather, is in the infirmity of the evidence itself. All the procedural protections in the world cannot save an innocent man from conviction if the substantive evidence against him appears overwhelming.

We are only just beginning to discover how problematic much seemingly strong evidence can be. In chapter 5, we will examine these limitations with respect to so-called forensic science, the crime scene investigation (CSI) evidence so extolled by television, movies, and the media generally. But first we should look at one of the most traditional forms of evidence: eyewitness testimony.

An eyewitness's identification of an accused defendant often provides some of the most dramatic and powerful evidence in a criminal case. "Do you see in this courtroom the person you saw fire the fatal shot?" asks the prosecutor. "Yes," says the eyewitness, pointing to the defendant, and adding for good measure, "I will never forget his face."

But in fact the eyewitness is frequently wrong. Indeed, in the case of some of the most serious crimes, murder and rape, inaccurate eyewitness identifications appear to be the single greatest contributor to wrongful convictions. These are the crimes that have been the particular focus of the Innocence Project, which has used DNA to help exonerate more than 360 individuals. Eyewitness identification was introduced as evidence in over 70 percent of these cases. Indeed, nearly a third of these cases involved multiple misidentifications of the defendant. By comparison, the next-most-frequent contributor to wrongful conviction, misleading testimony by forensic "experts" (discussed in chapter 5), was present in 45 percent of these cases, and the third-most-frequent factor, false confessions, was present in about 30 percent of them.

Of course, given jury secrecy, we cannot know for sure that it was wrongful eyewitness testimony that led to these wrongful convictions. And given that the total number of Innocence Project exonerations is fewer than four hundred and that the crimes involved were only the most serious, there are limits to how much of a general inference one can draw from the fact that wrongful eyewitness testimony was so common in such cases. But even in the much larger sample provided by the National Registry of Exonerations, involving (as noted in chapter 2) over 2,400 exonerations since 1989 for a wide variety of crimes, the percentage of cases in which erroneous eyewitness evidence was introduced was still a hefty 40 percent. And the inherently powerful nature of such evidence makes it more than reasonable to infer that erroneous eyewitness evidence played a material role in these hundreds of wrongful convictions.

While some eyewitnesses have had prior contact with the person they identify as the perpetrator of a crime (as when a neighbor sees a husband abusing his wife), many have had none: they see the defendant only once, when they witness the crime. But in some respects this makes their testimony stronger, for they have no motive to lie. The defendant is a complete stranger to them, and they simply had the misfortune to have been a passerby or, worse, a victim. In either case, the encounter was something they were not likely to forget—and it seems highly likely that the jury therefore found their testimony believable.

Yet the subsequent exonerations show, if nothing else, that these eyewitness identifications are frequently wrong. Why is this? Improper police practices sometimes play a part, as when a police officer conducting a lineup urges the eyewitness to "take a good look at number 3," or when the eyewitness only tentatively identifies the person in the lineup whom the officer suspects is the culprit and the officer says, "Good work." But the chief causes of inaccurate eyewitness identifications are shortcomings inherent in human perception and memory that cannot be eliminated easily, if at all. Some of these are obvious. The ability of an eyewitness to perceive the face of a culprit will be affected by lighting, by distance and angle, by the acuity of the eyewitness's eyesight, by the amount of time the eyewitness looked at the culprit, and by distractions such as a gun. Similarly, memories tend to fade over time, which may affect how accurately an eyewitness can remember a face seen many hours, days, or even weeks earlier.

Considerable research indicates that many people overrate their ability to perceive and remember faces they saw only once, and that what they remember mostly relates to some general characteristic, such as that the culprit was square-jawed or had a mustache. The research also shows that there are many less-than-obvious factors that may also influence and distort an eyewitness's perceptions and recollections. For instance, careful studies going back as far as the 1980s have demonstrated what is now called the other-race effect: Eyewitnesses are less likely to misidentify someone of their own race than they are to misidentify someone of another race. While theories vary as to *why* this is so, that it *is* so is now pretty much beyond dispute.

Another less-than-obvious factor is the tendency of memories to merge over time in order to fill the gaps. An eyewitness who does not know the identity of the perpetrator, say, will thus often be asked by police to view a lineup or a photo array that includes one or more possible suspects, to see if the eyewitness can pick out any of them as the culprit. At the time of this viewing, the eyewitness may have only a somewhat blurred memory of the crime but will typically study the lineup or photographs with care before making a selection (if any). By the time the eyewitness testifies at trial, however, the rough memory of the perpetrator from the actual time of the crime will often have merged with the memory formed from the much more careful scrutiny of the lineup or photographs, so that the eyewitness honestly thinks he remembers a particular detail, like a scar on the defendant's face, from the time of the crime, even though his perception of that detail came from his viewing of the lineup or photographs.

Common assumptions may also potentially distort an eyewitness identification. For example, even if a well-trained police officer makes a point of telling an eyewitness not to assume that any of the people being viewed in a lineup or photo array is a suspect, research suggests that most eyewitnesses will naturally assume that one or more suspects are indeed included, and this will increase the likelihood that the eyewitness will make an identification.

To be sure, not all police lineups and photo arrays are conducted with proper care and caution, and many of the legal developments of the last few decades regarding eyewitness identifications have focused on requiring less suggestive police procedures, such as having a lineup or photo array conducted by an officer not involved in the investigation of the crime. The purpose of this reform is to eliminate the possibility that the officer will suggest, if only through body language, that the eyewitness should make a particular selection. But such reforms, though salutary, are largely irrelevant to solving the more basic problems of human perception and memory that appear to be the main cause of so many false identifications.

Some of these misidentifications have been astonishing. Consider the following three cases:

- In 1984, Kirk Bloodsworth was convicted and sentenced to death for the rape and murder of a nine-year-old girl in Baltimore. While no physical or circumstantial evidence linked him to the crime, no fewer than five eyewitnesses placed him with the victim or at the scene of the crime. At the time, DNA testing had not yet made its way into the criminal justice system (the first U.S. case involving its use by prosecutors was in 1988, and defense lawyers did not begin to use it until a few years later). Finally, however, in 1993, DNA analysis of the semen extracted from the girl's underwear showed that the culprit was not Bloodsworth but someone else, who eventually confessed. Thankfully, Bloodsworth had not been executed, and he was set free that year.

- Also in 1984, a college student named Jennifer Thompson was raped in Burlington, North Carolina. When shown an array of six photos, she tentatively identified the one of a stranger named Ronald Cotton as her assailant, initially stating, "I think this is the guy." By the time of trial, however, Thompson testified that she was "absolutely sure" that Cotton was the man who had raped her. Cotton was convicted and sentenced to life imprisonment. Over a decade later, DNA testing of the semen taken from her vagina right after the crime proved to be that of another man, who was then charged, and Cotton was set free. (Remarkably, Thompson and Cotton have since reconciled, even bonded.)

- In 1974, James Bain was convicted in Florida of raping a nine-year-old boy. Although this was long before DNA testing was available, blood found in the semen taken from the boy's underwear was type B, and Bain's blood was type AB. Nevertheless, the jury convicted him, chiefly on the basis of the boy's identification of Bain, which he had consistently provided from the initial photo array through the trial. Years later, after DNA testing became available, Bain filed handwritten motions in court four times asking for DNA testing of the semen, but all four requests were denied. Finally, however, after Bain obtained assistance from a lawyer from the Innocence Project of Florida, DNA testing was granted—and it completely exonerated him. He was released in 2009, having served thirty-five years for a crime he did not commit.

In each of these cases, had it not been for DNA testing, the defendants would still be in prison, or dead. But DNA samples are either unavailable or irrelevant to the investigation and prosecution of most crimes. It may reasonably be inferred, therefore, that numerous defendants currently imprisoned were wrongly convicted on the basis of inaccurate eyewitness testimony. And it may be further assumed that while some of these inaccurate identifications may have been the product of suggestive police procedures, many more were the result of shortcomings in perception and memory that are endemic to the human species. Largely uncontrollable factors that may diminish the accuracy of eyewitness identifications include, among numerous other factors and in addition to the limitations already mentioned, (1) the eyewitness's own level of stress or trauma at the time of the underlying incident, (2) the inherent tendency of memory over time to add embellishments to enhance the completeness of the recollection or simply to accord with preexisting biases, and (3) the wide range among people in their ability to retrieve memories of events that lasted only a short time.

How should the legal system deal with such seemingly intractable problems? The fact that eyewitness identifications are often unreliable was recognized by the Supreme Court as early as 1967 in cases like *United States v. Wade, Gilbert v. California*, and *Stovall v. Denno*, which focused on the need to have defense counsel present at lineups in order to avoid unfairness. It was not until a decade later, in 1977, that the Supreme Court, in *Manson v. Brathwaite*, addressed the issue of whether eyewitness identifications might be the product of overly suggestive police techniques, such as, in *Manson*, showing the eyewitness a single photograph. The emphasis in *Manson* and in most subsequent cases was on identifying and eliminating such practices, since they were the aspect of eyewitness inaccuracy that could most readily be fixed.

Although much remains to be done in this regard, progress has been made. At least nine states now require that lineups and photo arrays be blindly administered (i.e., by a police officer who has no familiarity with the investiga tion). Many states and localities also require the police managing the lineups and photo arrays to read from a script that minimizes suggestiveness. Further still, eleven states now require that the eyewitness's initial degree of confidence in making an identification be recorded and made available to the defense. While further reforms are required—such as videotaping the suspects in the lineups (and perhaps the eyewitness reactions) and training the police who administer the lineups and photo arrays to avoid even unconscious suggestiveness—at least police procedure is an area in which concrete steps can be taken to minimize inaccuracy.

But neither the courts nor the police have done much to deal with the bigger problem of eyewitness inaccuracy caused by fundamental problems in an ordinary person's perception and memory. Although the *Manson* decision invited federal trial courts to exclude eyewitness testimony, not just for police suggestiveness but also for inherent infirmities, this invitation, coming as it did before most of the research on the less obvious weaknesses of perception and memory had been undertaken, has in practice rarely led to exclusion of eyewitness testimony on any basis other than improper police procedures. And indeed, it is hard to see how a trial judge (let alone a jury) could, for example, determine whether a given eyewitness's identification was unduly affected by stress at the time of perception, embellishment of memories over time, or the like.

More recently, however, a few state courts, most notably in New Jersey, have begun experimenting with a different approach: either instructing jurors about the limitations on human perception and memory that affect eyewitness identification or allowing experts to testify about them. The idea is not to comment on the specific eyewitness testimony presented in the case, but simply to alert the jury that as a general matter eyewitness testimony may not be as reliable as it appears to be. Regretfully, preliminary studies have concluded that the effectiveness of these approaches is modest. Jurors seem to interpret a judge's special instructions on the subject of eyewitness identification as a veiled message that the judge does not believe the eyewitness; they therefore do not simply reduce the weight they give to the eyewitness's testimony, but rather reject it altogether. Expert testimony, for its part, often devolves into a battle between experts on both sides, which, according to these studies, the jury resolves by simply ignoring the expert testimony. In both cases, the result is that jurors still do not undertake the admittedly difficult task of treating eyewitness testimony with great care and caution but not ignoring it entirely.

In my opinion, these approaches also ignore the fact that, as described in chapter 2, the overwhelming majority of criminal cases, both state and federal, are resolved by plea bargains or other dispositions not requiring any fact-finding by a judge or jury. Instead, resolving criminal cases has become primarily the responsibility of prosecutors, who now have nearly unfettered discretion to decide who shall be charged, what the charges will be, and how they should be resolved. While this is unfortunate, it is also unlikely to change in the near future. Thus, the best thing that can now be done to mitigate the frequent inaccuracy of eyewitness identifications is to educate prosecutors, through training early in their careers, about the dangers of eyewitness inaccuracy that persist even when police procedures have been unassailable. It may be that courts could not order such training (though the legislative and executive branches easily could), but the courts could suggest its adoption with an emphasis that might be persuasive.

One other modest mitigating factor should be mentioned. For many everyday crimes, like robbery, the presence of surveillance cameras in stores and buildings has made the police somewhat less dependent on eyewitness identification. The broader use of such surveillance cameras in public places should therefore be encouraged. Of course, this is only a partial solution, not only because those committing crimes often seek to avoid detection by, for example, wearing masks but also because it remains the case that a great many violent crimes are committed in private dwellings where state-ordered surveillance is largely forbidden by the Constitution and concerns for privacy.

Eyewitness identification thus presents the legal system with a challenge unlike any other. In many cases, the only direct evidence of who committed a crime is the testimony of an eyewitness. Yet modern science suggests that much of such testimony is inherently suspect—but not in ways that jurors can readily evaluate from their own experience. The result, alas, is a very real and continuing possibility of wrongful convictions based on inaccurate eyewitness identifications.

4

WILL THE DEATH PENALTY EVER DIE?

Although relatively few Americans are executed each year, the death penalty is an issue of considerable importance to many Americans, who treat it as symbolic of society's attitudes toward crime, punishment, and morality. But for me it also has a personal component. When my older brother Jan David Rakoff was murdered in 1985, bolts of anger and outrage not infrequently penetrated the black cloud of my grief. Though I knew almost nothing about Jan's confessed murderer except his name, I wished him dead.

My brother, at age forty-four, had just begun to come into his own. His innovative educational theories were starting to attract attention, and, just as important, he had come to terms with his homosexuality, which for many years he had struggled to suppress. While on a trip to Manila, he engaged the services of a male prostitute, but at the end they quarreled over money. In a fit of rage, the prostitute assaulted my brother with a pipe burner and an ice pick, bludgeoning and stabbing him to death. To cover his tracks, the attacker then set fire to the bungalow where my brother was staying; but the smoke attracted the attention of a security guard, who apprehended the fleeing assailant. Later that evening, the assailant provided a full written confession.

When my brother's body arrived back in the United States, his face and head were barely recognizable, so vicious had been the assault. My heart cried out for vengeance. Although the death penalty was then available in the Philippines, the defendant, taking full advantage of a corrupt legal system, negotiated a sentence of just three years in prison. Had, instead, the prosecutor recommended the death penalty, I would have applauded.

It took many years before I changed my mind.

Looking at the death penalty from the perspective of a judge, one cannot ignore the continued difficulties the Supreme Court has had in attempting to regulate capital punishment so that it conforms to constitutional standards. This, as well as the dismal history of the death penalty, has been the subject of much scholarly work. If I have a criticism of these mostly very able accounts, it is of their failure to give more than passing attention to the moral outrage that provides much of the emotional support for the death penalty—outrage felt not only by the family and friends of a murder victim but also by the many empathetic members of the public who, having learned the brutal facts of the murder, feel strongly that the murderer has forfeited his own right to live.

For many of the scholars, the debate over the death penalty is, first and foremost, a symbolic battle over cultural values, with a strong current of racism running just below the surface. This may well be true, but unless one acknowledges that rational human beings can feel such revulsion at the taking of an innocent life as to wish the taker dead, one cannot otherwise account for the somewhat paradoxical fact that, as many polls confirm, the death penalty continues to enjoy widespread popular support even in those states and countries that have banned it.

At the same time, it can hardly be denied that the death penalty is imposed in this country in a racially unjust manner. As fully documented, for example, in the recent history of the death penalty by law professors Carol Steiker and Jordan Steiker, titled *Courting Death*, throughout the nineteenth and twentieth centuries, and even now, death sentences are disproportionately imposed on Black men who commit crimes against whites, especially white women. Those who are actually executed are even more disproportionately men of color. While most states still permit the sentence of capital punishment (and the Trump administration has pursued it aggressively at the federal level), it is mainly in the South that executions take place, reflecting, in the Steikers' view, "the South's historical practice of chattel slavery and of slavery's enduring racial legacy."

The confinement of executions chiefly to the southern states is also the product of the South's history of violent racial tension. Legal executions aside, more than three thousand people were lynched in the South between 1880 and 1930, nearly all of them Black men, whereas there were comparatively few lynchings in the West and virtually none in the North. As the Steikers note, "One of the strongest predictors of a state's propensity to conduct executions today is its history of lynch mob activity more than a century ago."

Since the death penalty is primarily imposed on southern Black males, it is hardly surprising that the first successful attacks on capital punishment in the Supreme Court were led by the NAACP Legal Defense Fund. Somewhat ironically, however, the NAACP and its lawyers found that their most successful strategy was to attack capital punishment not so much on the ground that it was racially unjust, but rather on the ground that it was imposed in a way so lacking in standards as to be unconstitutionally arbitrary. It was on this ground that the Supreme Court, in *Furman v. Georgia* (1972), held the death penalty unconstitutional as then applied.

Although there was no single opinion in *Furman* that commanded a majority of the Court, the largest plurality of justices joined an opinion by Justice Potter Stewart that read in part as follows:

> These death sentences are cruel and unusual in the same way that being struck by lightning is cruel and unusual. For, of all the people convicted of rapes and murders in 1967 and 1968, many just as reprehensible as these, the petitioners are among a capriciously selected random handful upon whom the sentence of death has in fact been imposed. My concurring Brothers [Justices Thurgood Marshall and William O. Douglas] have demonstrated that, if any basis can be discerned for the selection of these few to be sentenced to die, it is the constitutionally impermissible basis of race. . . . But racial discrimination has not been proved, and I put it to one side. I simply conclude that the Eighth and Fourteenth Amendments cannot tolerate the infliction of a sentence of death under legal systems that permit this unique penalty to be so wantonly and so freakishly imposed.

Whatever its rationale, *Furman* suspended the death penalty—but not for long. Responding to Justice Stewart's opinion that the death penalty was unconstitutional because it was imposed in an arbitrary fashion, no fewer than thirty-five states, in the space of less than four years, enacted statutes supplying standards that supposedly would apply the death penalty in a nonarbitrary way.

In 1976, in the case of *Gregg v. Georgia*, the Supreme Court upheld these laws, and capital punishment was restored.

Since then and until fairly recently, the history of the death penalty in the Supreme Court has largely been a matter of reviewing and refining these standards, which in most jurisdictions take the form of "aggravating" and "mitigating" factors that a judge or jury must consider in deciding whether or not to impose the death penalty. This "regulatory" approach has been something of a disaster. For one thing, the Supreme Court has mandated that the standards not be so rigid or precise as to deprive judges and juries of meaningful discretion to take account of the particulars of each case. But this in turn has led the Court to approve broad and vague standards that, in practice, accord judges and juries the same unfettered discretion that led to the problem of arbitrariness that the plurality in *Furman* condemned.

For example, a common aggravating factor that a judge or jury is supposed to consider in deciding whether to impose the death penalty on someone convicted of murder is whether the defendant committed the murder in the course of committing some other crime. But the list of such other crimes—typically including rape, robbery, burglary, and assault—is frequently so all-encompassing as to apply to the great majority of situations in which murders are committed. So this factor does little to meaningfully limit or define the exercise of discretion. Another common aggravating factor is that the defendant exhibited "utter disregard for human life" when he committed the murder. How many murderers cannot be fit into this category? And doesn't this mean that, in practice, imposition of the death penalty is still effectively standardless?

Moreover, litigation over the wording and application of these standards, coupled with many judges' growing discomfort with the death penalty, has led to years-long delays between the imposition of the death penalty and the actual execution. This has effectively deprived the death penalty of much of the supposed retributive and deterrent force that, as the Supreme Court held in *Gregg*, justified its imposition.

As noted by Justice Stephen Breyer, dissenting in the case of *Glossip v. Gross* (2015), these "unconscionably long delays . . . undermine the death penalty's penological purpose." Even Congress's attempt in 1996 to reduce such delays through the Antiterrorism and Effective Death Penalty Act (AEDPA) has proved totally ineffective in this respect (though, as discussed in chapter 9, AEDPA has had the terrible collateral effect of largely eliminating meaningful federal review of state violations of defendants' rights in noncapital cases). In part this is because anti–death penalty lawyers from many large and sophisticated law firms have contributed very substantial free services to challenging executions (e.g., by challenging the method of execution, such as by injection, as cruel and unusual). But it also reflects the fact that federal judges, notwithstanding the limits on review of state cases imposed by AEDPA, recognize that a decision to deny a challenge to an imminent execution is the functional equivalent of ordering the defendant's immediate death, and will often pause before taking such an irreversible step. Thus, despite AEDPA, the time between imposition of the death penalty and actual execution is now, on average, fifteen years.

Further still, the costs of defending all this litigation and delay, as well as housing defendants in specially designed death-row facilities, are chiefly borne not by the federal or even state governments, but by local communities. And these costs are often huge, in some cases actually threatening to bankrupt the locality and in others diverting much-needed resources away from the rest of law enforcement. A state commission in California, for example, has determined that when one adds up the costs to the state and to local municipalities in California of litigating death penalty cases through their complicated proceedings, incarcerating the defendants in separate death-row facilities, constructing and maintaining execution chambers, and arranging for all the other special features of a death penalty case, the expense to the public of operating a death penalty system in California is more than ten times what the cost would be if the defendants were sentenced instead to life imprisonment without parole.

In short, the Supreme Court's regulatory approach has proved endlessly slow, immensely expensive, counterproductive to the supposed purposes of the death penalty, and nearly as arbitrary as the system it replaced.

More recently, the Court has also begun to impose some limitations on the death penalty by holding it unconstitutional when applied to adolescents and to mentally disabled persons. While these decisions are partly based on the neuroscience data discussed in chapter 6, they are chiefly premised on what the Court's majority perceives to be a national consensus on such issues, a rationale that seems unlikely to apply to capital punishment as a whole. Inevitably, these decisions have also engendered their own litigation—for example, over what tests can properly be applied to determine if a defendant is mentally disabled.

Polls do suggest, however, that while a majority of Americans still favor the death penalty, they do so less strongly than they once did. But this does not appear to be a function of the regulatory problems discussed above. Partly it is a result of declining crime and murder rates. It can also be attributed to the by now overwhelming evidence that the death penalty has been imposed in dozens, if not hundreds, of cases in which it was ultimately proved that the defendants were actually innocent.

The discovery that we were executing, or coming perilously close to executing, scores of wholly innocent people was originally the work of the Innocence Project and its innovative use of DNA testing in cases, such as rape-related murders, in which samples of bodily fluids or tissues had been retained long after the convictions. In many such cases, DNA testing disclosed that the semen removed from the victim of a rape-murder was not that of the death-row defendant convicted of the crime, but rather of some other suspect whom the police had chosen not to pursue.

Other organizations eventually joined the Innocence Project in reopening closed cases, with the result that, according to a list maintained by the National Registry of Exonerations (discussed in chapter 2), dozens of defendants convicted of death-eligible offenses have now been completely exonerated by the courts, many after having spent years on death row. We can only imagine how many of the defendants who were actually executed were similarly innocent, but one widely accepted study puts the figure at no less than 4 percent.

It should also be noted that the main reasons for the wrongful convictions in death-eligible cases were inaccurate eyewitness identifications, perjured testimony, and flawed evidence from forensic experts (as discussed briefly in chapter 3 and in chapter 5 to come). These problems are endemic to the current U.S. criminal justice system but not meaningfully addressed in any of the Supreme Court's death penalty decisions.

The exonerations already registered may constitute only a small percentage of the exonerations yet to come. At present, testing for DNA can yield definitive results only in cases in which the crime scene evidence consists of DNA mixtures from no more than two people, and in many cases no crime scene DNA samples are available at all. But much work has already been done toward developing effective ways to assess DNA samples containing the DNA of three or four or even more persons—so that, for example, one can determine who was, or was not, involved in a gang rape or in an assault with a firearm handled by several persons. Although these methodologies may not yet be sufficiently reliable to warrant their use in court, greater reliability is coming—and its development will doubtless provide proof leading to new exonerations (and new convictions). Similarly, fingerprint evidence, which in its current form is somewhat unreliable because of the large measure of subjectivity involved in its interpretation, has been the subject of much recent work to improve its accuracy in ways that may likewise lead to further exonerations.

But what good are all these future possibilities of reliable exonerations if the defendants have already been put to death? It was on this basis that in 2002, in *United States v. Quinones*, I declared the federal death penalty unconstitutional. Specifically, I held that under the due process clause of the Constitution, an innocent person never loses his legal right to prove his innocence, but that he has been effectively deprived of that right if he is executed.

My decision was promptly reversed by a panel of the Second Circuit Court of Appeals, which, wrongly in my view, interpreted a 1993 Supreme Court case, *Herrera v. Collins*, as holding that even an innocent defendant eventually loses his right to be exonerated by proving his innocence (even though the critical fifth vote for the majority in *Herrera*, by Justice Sandra Day O'Connor, expressly stated the contrary). But because of that interpretation, the Steikers, after kindly mentioning my decision in their book, conclude that "powerful as the innocence issue may be as a policy concern, the lack of precedent supporting the argument likely undermines its use as the sole ground for a constitutional attack on the death penalty."

Perhaps they are right. But it still seems to me that the execution or near execution of the innocent is the factor most likely to deprive the death penalty of its moral force and thereby its ultimate legal justification. Nor is this just my opinion. In *The Making of a Justice*, the memoir that John Paul Stevens published just two months before his death in 2019, the former, great Supreme Court Justice wrote: "When the Supreme Court reviewed the constitutionality of the death penalty at length in 1976, none of us seriously considered the magnitude of the risk of error in capital cases. It is now perfectly clear that it is a risk that no civilized society should tolerate." For how can one applaud capital punishment knowing that those executed may well be innocent? One can only wonder how many more wrongly convicted innocent people will have to go to the death chamber before these ingrained attitudes will change for others, as they did for me.

5

THE FAILURES, AND FUTURE, OF FORENSIC SCIENCE

Although, as discussed in chapter 3, eyewitness identification evidence may be far more problematic than most people realize, anyone who watches crime shows knows that twenty-first-century police and prosecutors now have at their disposal an array of modern forensic techniques—including not just DNA testing and traditional fingerprint comparison but also hair analysis, fiber analysis, paint analysis, clothing analysis, firearm analysis, bloodstain analysis, and even bite-mark analysis—that can scientifically establish guilt or innocence. Or can they? In actuality, it has become increasingly apparent that, with the exception of DNA testing, most of these techniques are unscientific, involve a great deal of disguised guesswork, and too frequently result in false convictions. Thus, of the more than 2,400 proven false convictions since 1989 recorded by the National Registry of Exonerations, nearly 600, or 25 percent, involved false or misleading forensic evidence.

The precursors of most of the forensic techniques used today were originally developed by police labs as helpful investigative tools, with no claim to being serious science. But, starting in the first quarter of the twentieth century, the information obtained by use of these tools was introduced as substantive evidence in criminal cases by lab technicians (or sometimes ordinary police officers) portrayed as highly qualified "forensic experts." These "experts," few of whom had extensive scientific training, nonetheless commonly testified that their conclusions had been reached to "a reasonable degree of scientific certainty"—a catchphrase that increasingly became the key to the admissibility of their testimony in court. Such testimony went largely uncontested by defense counsel, who lacked the scientific and technical training to challenge it.

This began to change somewhat, beginning in the late 1980s, when DNA testing was developed by scientists applying rigorous standards, independently of the criminal justice system. It proved to be far more reliable in establishing guilt or innocence than any of the forensic techniques that preceded it. DNA testing not only helped to convict the guilty but also led to the exoneration of hundreds of felons, many of whom had been convicted on the basis of faulty forensic evidence.

The leader in this has been the Innocence Project, founded in 1992 by Peter Neufeld and Barry Scheck at Cardozo Law School. As noted in chapter 3, the Innocence Project has used DNA testing to prove in court that more than 360 people who had been convicted of such serious crimes as murder and rape (and had served an average of fourteen years in prison) were actually innocent. In over 40 percent of these cases, forensic science testimony that had been introduced at the underlying trials to "prove" the defendants were guilty was shown by the subsequent DNA testing to be flatly wrong. In effect, DNA testing, because it was so good, exposed how bad much other forensic evidence was.

On the heels of the introduction of DNA testing into the criminal justice system, the Supreme Court, in 1993, gave federal judges the responsibility to act as gatekeepers for the admissibility of scientific and other forensic testimony. Previously, both state and federal judges had determined the admissibility of such testimony by applying the so-called *Frye* test, named after the 1923 decision of the U.S. Court of Appeals for the D.C. Circuit in *Frye v. United States*. *Frye* held that, to be admissible, the expert's opinions had to be "deduced from a well-recognized scientific principle or discovery . . . sufficiently established to have gained general acceptance in the particular field in which it belongs."

In the *Frye* case, the court, applying this standard, held that polygraph (lie-detector) evidence was not sufficiently accepted as reliable to allow its admissibility in federal court, and this remains true today. But in other instances, the "general acceptance" standard proved elusive. For example, if most fingerprint examiners were of the view that fingerprint comparison was a reliable technique that enabled them to reach results with a reasonable degree of scientific certainty, did this mean that it had "general acceptance in the particular field in which it belongs"? Most courts came to answer yes, and as a result the *Frye* standard proved to be little or no impediment to the introduction of most kinds of forensic evidence.

However, the Supreme Court, in the civil case *Daubert v. Merrell Dow Pharmaceuticals Inc.* (1993), overrode the *Frye* test. The Court held that federal judges had to take a much more engaged approach to the admissibility of scientific (and other expert) testimony, so as, in effect, to weed out junk science. Under this new standard, a judge, in order to rule on the admissibility of purported scientific testimony, had to examine whether the methodology it reflected not only was generally accepted but also had been subject to scientific testing, had been peer-reviewed in respected scientific journals, and had a known and low error rate. The result was a much more searching inquiry by the gate-keeper judge—or so the Court intended.

Initially, this intention was not realized in criminal cases—even though *Daubert* was so clearly an improvement over *Frye* that its standards were eventually adopted, in whole or in part, by thirty-eight states. But in these jurisdictions, while *Daubert* challenges to expert scientific testimony were successful in a notable percentage of civil cases, they almost never succeeded in criminal cases.

One reason for this is money. Most criminal defense counsel lack expertise when it comes to science (as do most judges); to mount a successful *Daubert* challenge, they need to hire a scientific expert. But most criminal defendants are indigent, and while they are given counsel at state expense, many jurisdictions do not provide additional funding for the employment of forensic experts. Furthermore, even in those jurisdictions where such funding is in principle available, many courts are stingy in their approval of funds for these purposes.

Beyond this, another barrier to the successful challenge of forensic testimony offered by the government in criminal cases is the unconscious bias of many judges in favor of admitting such evidence. This may be especially true in state courts, where the great majority of criminal cases are brought. Many, perhaps most, state judges assigned to hear criminal cases are former prosecutors who, in their prior careers, regularly introduced such questionable forensic science.

Furthermore, in most states criminal court judges are elected and cannot afford to be known as "soft on crime" if they want to be reelected. Anecdotal evidence also suggests that some state judges are sensitive to jurors' expectations that the government will offer the kind of crime lab or CSI evidence the jurors have seen on television, and that depriving the prosecution of such evidence may seriously impede the prosecution's case. When to all these tendencies and pressures there is added the sheer fact that in most states the criminal court judges are overloaded with cases and can only with difficulty find the time to undertake a truly probing *Daubert* hearing, it is hardly surprising that successful challenges to forensic evidence in criminal cases are rare and often denied on the most cursory grounds.

Nevertheless, the large number of DNA exonerations eventually convinced many thoughtful people that forensic testimony deserved greater scrutiny. In late 2005, Congress directed the National Academy of Sciences (NAS) to study the problem. The result was a 352-page report issued in 2009—prepared by a distinguished committee of scientists, academics, and practitioners, and co-chaired by federal appellate judge Harry T. Edwards—titled *Strengthening Forensic Science in the United States: A Path Forward.*

The report was highly critical of hitherto accepted forensic techniques such as microscopic hair matching, bite-mark matching, fiber matching, handwriting comparisons, toolmark analysis, shoeprint and tire track analysis, and bloodstain analysis. Its repeated criticisms were that little or no rigorous scientific testing had been done to determine the validity and reliability of these techniques and that their application was, in practice, highly subjective. Even fingerprint analysis—which until the advent of DNA testing had been considered the gold standard in forensic evidence—did not escape criticism. The report noted that it had never been the subject of rigorous independent testing by trained scientists, and the differences and deficiencies in its application by its practitioners often yielded inconsistent results.

In one notorious case, a fingerprint found on a bag of detonators connected to the 2004 train bombings in Madrid was sent by the Spanish authorities to fingerprint databases throughout the world. In response, the FBI announced that its experts had determined that the source of the fingerprint was an Oregon attorney named Brandon Mayfield. Although the Spanish authorities were skeptical, the FBI dispatched one of its experts to Spain to try to change their minds. Meanwhile, the FBI obtained authority to conduct covert twenty-four-hour electronic surveillance of Mayfield. And when, in early May 2004, the government somehow imagined that he might flee, it obtained court approval to arrest and detain him. It also obtained warrants to search his home, office, and vehicles.

Two weeks later, however, with Mayfield still in jail (though charged with no crime), the Madrid authorities announced that their own experts had concluded that the fingerprint belonged to a different person, Ouhnane Daoud. Mayfield was released from jail, and the FBI, after several more days of haggling with the Spanish officials, finally admitted that its conclusion that the fingerprint on the detonator definitely matched Mayfield's was erroneous.

Why did the FBI get it wrong? A subsequent investigation by the Department of Justice's inspector general found that many factors were involved, including bias, circular reasoning, and a reluctance to admit errors. But as the NAS report noted, these deficiencies could never have played a part were it not for the fact that subjectivity is intrinsic to fingerprint analysis. And where there is a high degree of subjectivity involved in reaching a conclusion, mistakes are inevitable.

To be sure, the problems the NAS report found with fingerprint analysis were nothing compared to the problems it found with most other forms of forensic science. It concluded: "Much forensic evidence—including, for example, bite marks and firearm and toolmark identifications—is introduced in criminal trials without any meaningful scientific validation, determination of error rates, or reliability testing to explain the limits of the discipline."

The main recommendation of the NAS report was the creation of an independent federal forensic institute to rigorously test the various methodologies and set standards for their application. Although, in my view, this would have been an ideal solution, the recommendation was opposed by a variety of special interests, ranging from the Department of Justice (DOJ) to local police organizations and private forensic labs. Nevertheless, in response to embarrassments like the Mayfield incident, as well as continuing expressions of concern from Congress, the DOJ —in collaboration with the Department of Commerce, which oversees what used to be called the Bureau of Standards and is now called the National Institute of Standards and Technology (NIST)—agreed in 2013 to create the National Commission on Forensic Science (NCFS) to recommend improvements in the handling of forensic science.

The NCFS's thirty-one members represented virtually every interest group concerned with forensic science, including prosecutors, defense counsel, scientists, forensic science practitioners, lab directors, law professors, and state court judges. (The commission also included, ex officio, one federal judge—me.) The idea was to reach consensus among all the relevant participants wherever possible. To this end, the NCFS required that two-thirds of its members had to vote in favor of a recommendation in order to send it to the government.

Over the four years of its existence, from 2013 to 2017, the NCFS made more than forty recommendations to the DOJ, which accepted most, though not all, of them. For example, over 80 percent of the commissioners approved a resolution that forensic experts should no longer testify that their opinions were given with "a reasonable degree of scientific [or other forensic discipline] certainty," because "such terms have no scientific meaning and may mislead jurors or judges" into thinking the forensic evidence is much stronger and scientific than it actually is. But although the DOJ accepted that recommendation, and thus made it binding on forensic experts called by federal prosecutors, many states still permit this highly misleading formulation and some even require it before allowing a forensic expert to testify.

As this illustrates, the NCFS's work did not have as much impact on the states as its members had hoped it might. Some states either ignored or expressed disagreement with its recommendations even when they were adopted on the federal level by the DOJ. Many police-sponsored forensic laboratories, in particular, viewed much of the NCFS's work as an attack on their integrity rather than an effort to improve their methodology. The NCFS's recommendations received the most positive response in places where forensic lab scandals had made communities open to change. For example, in Houston, Texas, a series of shoddy and even dishonest practices by the police crime lab had been exposed. These culminated in 2014 when one of the lab's DNA technicians, who had worked on 185 criminal cases, including 51 murders, was found not only to have used improper procedures but also to have fabricated results and falsely tampered with official records—all seemingly to help convict defendants the police were "sure" were guilty. In response, the city created a new forensic lab, the Houston Forensic Science Center, entirely independent of the police and widely regarded as a model for the future, but still very much the exception to forensic labs in most municipalities.

The NCFS faced still another difficulty. The broad spectrum of interests represented in it, and the requirement that it proceed by something close to consensus, meant that it could not easily address the two fundamental problems with most forensic science identified by the NAS report: the lack of rigorous testing and the concomitant presence of a significant degree of subjectivity in reaching results. Nevertheless, the NCFS was attempting to begin addressing these problems—in particular, the issue of error rate—when its term expired in April 2017. Although a majority of the commissioners asked that its term be renewed so that these questions could be addressed, the new administration's DOJ flatly rejected the idea, claiming that it could proceed better through internally generated improvements.

In the view of many observers, the record so far invites skepticism about this claim. The first official product of the DOJ's internal Forensic Science Research and Development Working Group, issued in November 2018, was a set of new uniform terms for forensic testimony and reporting by federal forensic experts. Although many members of the NCFS and others had urged that experts avoid making categorical statements such as "the markings on the bullet found at the scene of the crime and the marking on the inside of the barrel of the gun found in the defendant's apartment came from the same source"—as opposed to more nuanced statements reflecting probabilities, error rates, and subjective choices—the DOJ imposed on its experts the categorical approach. In the words of Simon A. Cole, a professor of criminology, law, and society at the University of California at Irvine who has closely monitored the DOJ's policies, its new standard is "neither logical, nor scientific," and suggests that the department is "reversing progress toward improving forensic science in the U.S."

The obvious reason why the DOJ opted for the categorical approach is that it is more effective with juries. This illustrates the heart of the problem of leaving forensic science improvements to police and prosecutors. However much they might sincerely wish to improve forensic science, as police and prosecutors they are subject to the kinds of cognitive biases that bedevil good science. In other words, their desire to obtain results that will support the convictions of those they independently believe are guilty will cause them to overlook shortcomings in their current methodologies, remain skeptical of improvements, and be critical of any suggestion that their approach is biased, unscientific, or flawed.

There is one earlier development worth mentioning. Shortly before the end of the Obama administration, in September 2016, the President's Council of Advisors on Science and Technology (PCAST), a group of the nation's leading scientists that, since 2001, had advised the White House on scientific matters, issued a report to the president titled *Forensic Science in Criminal Courts: Ensuring Scientific Validity of Feature-Comparison Methods.*

The report began by surveying the data that showed just how weak much forensic science is, even by the government's standards. A good example is microscopic hair analysis, by which an expert claims to determine whether human hairs found at the scene of a crime uniquely match the hair of the accused. According to the report:

> Starting in 2012, the Department of Justice (DOJ) and FBI undertook an unprecedented review of testimony in more than 3,000 criminal cases involving microscopic hair analysis. Their initial results, released in 2015, showed that FBI examiners had provided scientifically invalid testimony in more than 95 percent of cases where that testimony was used to inculpate a defendant at trial.

How could this be? A recent example illustrates what can happen. In a decision handed down on March 1, 2019, the Court of Appeals for the D.C. Circuit reversed the 1972 murder and rape conviction of John Milton Ausby, describing in some detail how, at his trial, an FBI agent purporting to be a "microscopic hair analysis specialist," testified that hairs exhibit characteristics "unique to a particular individual" and that the hairs found on the victim's body and in her apartment were "microscopically identical" to Ausby's hair. But, stated the court, "the government now concedes that the testimony of the forensic expert was false and misleading and that the government knew or should have known so at the time of Ausby's trial." In other words, the agent effectively lied, and the government knowingly or negligently allowed him to do so. While the FBI must be given credit for its subsequent review of these egregious errors, that did not happen until 2012, forty years after Ausby's conviction. And even though it admitted these errors, the DOJ judged them to be immaterial, opposed Ausby's release, and sought a new trial. His conviction was not actually vacated until late 2019, by which time he had served forty-seven years in prison.

Overall, the PCAST report concluded, as had the NAS report, that most forensic science suffers from a lack of rigorous testing and an excess of subjectivity that makes it unreliable. Since, however, Congress has not pursued the NAS report's recommendation that an independent federal forensic institute be established, the PCAST report suggested that the NIST undertake scientific studies "to assess the foundational validity of current and newly developed forensic feature-comparison technologies." The NIST was thought to be the next best option because it had much less of a stake in the outcome of such studies than the DOJ, let alone state and private labs.

The PCAST report was met with severe criticism, notably from the FBI and local police authorities, who were loath to admit that the forensic science they used all the time was as fundamentally suspect as the report found. More important, the change in administration meant that the report and its recommendations were largely shelved, although the NIST has continued to do some helpful work on narrower issues. The new administration also constrained the role of PCAST, replaced many of its members with persons drawn from industry, and largely left it dormant.

One possible exception to the lack of progress may yet come from the federal judiciary. The PCAST report was critical—in my view, correctly—of the failure of most federal judges to undertake meaningful review of the admissibility of forensic science, notwithstanding that *Daubert* effectively mandates that they do so. The PCAST report therefore suggested that the overall federal judiciary, through its own advisory committees and educational arms, encourage federal judges to be more involved in such cases and provide guidance to these judges on how to do so. The recommendations relating to forensic science are currently (in 2020) being considered by the relevant committees of the federal judiciary. In particular, these committees are focusing on whether to require federal prosecutors to disclose to defense counsel well in advance of trial not only the government's forensic experts' opinions but also what data and methods its experts relied on in reaching their opinions.

There has also been some progress in some state courts. In New York, in particular, new legislation requires that the prosecutor reveal, quite soon after indictment, the bases for any forensic expert testimony that the prosecutor intends to introduce. And while the lower New York courts are still divided over just how far this disclosure must go, preliminary reports suggest that, even though New York is one of the few states that still adheres to the *Frye* standard, the fuller and earlier disclosure mandated by the new law has already led defense counsel to make notably more challenges to forensic science than was true in the past.

Separately, I suggest that there are steps that could be taken to improve forensic science now, without undue expense or hassle:

1. Forensic labs could be made more independent of police and prosecutors' offices. Instead of being viewed as partners of the police and prosecutors, they could develop an ethos of objectivity and independence.

2. All forensic science labs, including private ones, could be made subject to state and federal accreditation requirements. An ethics code for forensic experts, already drafted by the NCFS and partly accepted by the DOJ, could also be made binding and enforceable on all such labs.

3. Testing by forensic labs could be made "blind," that is, free from any biasing information supplied by the police or other investigating authorities.

4. The courts could make greater use of court-appointed, comparatively neutral experts in place of the less-than-neutral experts chosen by the parties. Federal law already allows federal courts to appoint such experts, but the judges very rarely have done so.

5. Courts could reduce the judge-made barriers to collateral (post-appeal) review of criminal convictions in which doubtful forensic testimony played a part. For example, many states deny defendants the right to argue that their convictions were the result of deficient forensic testimony if they did not challenge these deficiencies at trial—even though the deficiencies may only have become known many years later. By contrast, courts in Texas, in response to some of the scandals mentioned earlier, now allow such challenges.

None of these steps would approach in significance the more far-reaching proposal made by the NAS report: the creation of an independent federal forensic institute to do the basic testing and promulgate the basic standards that would make forensic science much more genuinely scientific. But, as noted above, there are a variety of special interests opposed to such an institute; and until public opinion forces their hand, the more modest steps outlined above may be the best we can do.

Meanwhile, forensic techniques that in their origins were simply viewed as aids to police investigations have taken on an importance in the criminal justice system that they cannot honestly support. Their results are portrayed to judges, juries, prosecutors, and defense counsel as having a degree of validity and reliability that they simply do not have. Maybe fictional crime shows can live with such lies, but our criminal justice system should not.

6

BRAIN SCIENCE AND THE LAW—UNCOMFORTABLE BEDFELLOWS

As you sit reading this, you probably experience an internal voice, unheard by any outsider, that verbally repeats the words you see on the page. That voice (which, in your case, speaks perfect English) is part of what we call your conscious mind. And the physical organ that causes what you see on the page to be simultaneously voiced internally is what we call your brain. The scientific study of how the brain relates to the mind is what we call cognitive neuroscience.

The brain is an incredibly complex organ, and for most of modern history it has defied serious scientific study. But the development in the past few decades of various technologies that enable us to observe certain operations of the brain, collectively called brain scans, has considerably increased our knowledge of how brain activities correlate with various mental states and behaviors.

The law, for its part, is deeply concerned with mental states, particularly intentions, and how they relate to behavior. As Justice

Oliver Wendell Holmes, Jr., famously put it, "Even a dog distinguishes between being stumbled over and being kicked." Distinctions of intent frequently determine, as a matter of law, the difference between going to prison and going free. Cognitive neuroscience holds out the promise of helping us to perceive, decide, and explain how intentions are arrived at and carried out. In theory, therefore, cognitive neuroscience could have a huge impact on the development and refinement of the law.

But there is reason to pause. Cognitive neuroscience is still in its infancy, and much of what has so far emerged that might be relevant to the law consists largely of hypotheses that are far from certainties. The natural impulse of forward-thinking people to employ the wonders of neuroscience in making the law more "modern" and "scientific" needs to be tempered with a healthy skepticism, or some dire results are likely. Indeed, the history of using "brain science" to alter the law is not a pretty picture. A few examples will illustrate the point.

In the early twentieth century, a leading "science" was eugenics, which put forward, among other ideas, a genetic theory about the brain. Eugenics also had philosophical accompaniments similar to social Darwinism (and, coincidentally, was first developed by Darwin's half cousin, Francis Galton). Eugenicists claimed to "prove" that certain deleterious mental states, most notably "feeblemindedness," were directly inheritable. It followed that the frequency of such unfortunate states of mind could be greatly reduced by prohibiting the carriers of the defective genes from procreating. Not only would this be advantageous to society as a whole, but it would also reduce the number of people destined to a life of misery and dependency because of their feeblemindedness.

So convincing was this argument, and so attractive its "scientific" basis, that eugenics quickly won the support of a great many famous people across the political spectrum, including Alexander Graham Bell, Winston Churchill, W.E.B. Du Bois, Havelock Ellis, Herbert Hoover, John Maynard Keynes, Linus Pauling, Theodore Roosevelt, Margaret Sanger, and George Bernard Shaw. Many of the major universities in the United States included a eugenics course in their curriculum.

The widespread acceptance of eugenics also prepared the way for the enactment of state laws that permitted the forced sterilization of women thought to be carriers of "feeblemindedness." At first such laws were controversial, but in 1927 they were held constitutional by a nearly unanimous Supreme Court in the infamous case of *Buck v. Bell*. Writing for the eight justices in the majority (including such notables as Louis D. Brandeis, Harlan F. Stone, and William Howard Taft), Justice Oliver Wendell Holmes, Jr., found, in effect, that the Virginia state legislature was justified in concluding (based on eugenics) that imbecility was directly heritable, and that the findings of the court in the case showed that not just Carrie Buck but also her mother and illegitimate child were imbecilic. It was therefore entirely lawful to sterilize Buck against her will, because, in Holmes's words, "Three generations of imbeciles are enough."

In the first half of the twentieth century, more than fifty thousand Americans were sterilized on the basis of eugenics-based laws. It was not until Adolf Hitler became a prominent advocate of eugenics, praising it in *Mein Kampf* and repeatedly invoking it as a justification for his extermination of Jews, Gypsies, and gays, that the doubtful science behind eugenics began to be subjected to widespread criticism.

Yet even as eugenics began to be discredited in the 1940s, a new kind of "brain science" began to gain legal acceptance: lobotomies. A lobotomy is a surgical procedure that cuts the connections between the prefrontal cortex (the part of the brain most associated with cognition) and the rest of the brain (including the parts more associated with emotions). From the outset of its development in the 1930s, it was heralded as a way to rid patients of chronic obsessions, delusions, and other serious mental problems; indeed, many such results were initially reported. It was also regarded as the product of serious science, to the point that its originator, the Portuguese neurologist António Egas Moniz, shared the Nobel Prize for Medicine in 1949 in recognition of its development.

Lobotomy science was so widely accepted that in the United States alone at least forty thousand lobotomies were performed between 1940 and 1965. While most of these were not court-ordered, the law, accepting lobotomies as sound science, required only the most minimal consent on the part of the patient; often the patient was a juvenile and the "consent" was provided by the patient's parents. Lobotomies were also performed on homosexuals, who, in what was the official position of the American psychiatric community until 1973, suffered from a serious mental disorder by virtue of their sexual orientation.

Nonetheless, some drawbacks to lobotomies were, or should have been, evident from the outset. About 5 percent of those who underwent the operation died as a result. A much larger percentage were rendered, in effect, human vegetables, with a limited emotional life and decreased cognition. But many of these negative results were kept secret. For example, it was not until John F. Kennedy ran for president that it became widely known that his sister Rosemary had become severely mentally incapacitated as a result of the lobotomy performed on her in 1941, at her father's behest, when she was twenty-three years old.

Still, by the early 1960s, enough of the bad news had seeped out that lobotomies began to be subject to public scrutiny and legal limitations. Eventually, most nations banned lobotomies altogether; but they are still legal in the United States and some other countries in limited circumstances.

While U.S. law in the mid-twentieth century tolerated lobotomies, it positively embraced psychiatry in general and Freudian psychoanalysis in particular. This was hardly surprising, since, according to Professor Jeffrey Lieberman, former president of the American Psychiatric Association, "by 1960, almost every major psychiatry position in the country was occupied by a psychoanalyst" and, in turn, "the psychoanalytic movement had assumed the trappings of a religion." In the judicial establishment, the original high priest of this religion was the brilliant and highly influential federal appellate judge David L. Bazelon.

Having himself undergone psychoanalysis, Bazelon, for the better part of the 1950s and 1960s, sought to introduce Freudian concepts and reasoning into the law. For example, in his 1963 opinion in a robbery case called *Miller v. United States*, Bazelon, quoting from Freud's article "Psychoanalysis and the Ascertaining of Truth in Courts of Law," suggested that judges and juries should not infer a defendant's consciousness of guilt from the fact that the defendant, confronted by a victim with evidence that he had stolen a wallet, tried to flee the scene. Rather, said Bazelon, "Sigmund Freud [has] warned the legal profession [that] 'you may be led astray . . . by a neurotic who reacts as though he were guilty even though he is innocent.'" If Freud said it, it must be right.

Eventually, much of the analysis Bazelon used to introduce Freudian notions into the law proved both unworkable as law and unprovable as science, and some of his most important rulings based on such analysis were eventually discarded, sometimes with his own concurrence.

Ultimately, Bazelon himself became disenchanted with psychoanalysis. In a 1974 address to the American Psychiatric

Association, he denounced certain forms of psychiatric testimony as "wizardry" and added that "in no case is it more difficult to elicit productive and reliable expert testimony than in cases that call on the knowledge and practice of psychiatry." But this change of attitude of Bazelon, and others, came too late to be of much use to the hundreds of persons who had been declared incompetent, civilly committed to asylums, or otherwise deprived of their rights on the basis of what Bazelon subsequently denounced as "conclusory statements couched in psychiatric terminology" (a form of testimony that persists to this day in many court proceedings).

Still a more recent example of how the law has been misled by what previously passed for good brain science must be mentioned, since it bears on the conviction of innocent persons described in previous chapters. Beginning in the 1980s, a growing number of prominent psychotherapists advocated suggestive techniques to help their patients "recover" supposedly repressed memories of past traumas, such as childhood incestuous rapes. Eventually, in the early 1990s, more than a hundred people were prosecuted in the United States for sexual abuse based on such retrieved memories, and even though in most of these cases there was little or no other evidence, more than a quarter of the accused were convicted.

But also beginning in the early 1990s, careful studies undertaken by memory experts, most prominently Professor Elizabeth Loftus, showed that many of the techniques used in helping people to recover repressed memories had the ability to implant false memories in them, thus casting doubt on the entire enterprise. Although at first met with resistance, the work of Loftus and other serious scientists was so rigorous and convincing that it prevailed in the end. But while many of those convicted on the basis of recovered memory evidence were then released, others were not, and some may still be in prison.

It is only fair to note that, just as the law has often been too quick to embrace, and too slow to abandon, the accepted brain science of the moment, it is equally the case that the law has sometimes asked of brain scientists more than they are equipped to deliver. Consider, for example, the process of civil commitment, by which persons with serious mental disorders are involuntarily confined to psychiatric wards, mental facilities, insane asylums, and the like. Although these facilities (many of which have now been shut down) are in some respects like prisons, especially since the patients are not free to leave the premises and must follow the orders of their keepers, commitment to these facilities differs from commitment to prison in that the committed individuals are confined for an indefinite period (sometimes forever) until their treatment is sufficiently successful as to warrant their release. Moreover, the commitment comes about not by their being criminally convicted by a jury on proof beyond a reasonable doubt, but rather by a judge making a determination—almost exclusively on the basis of psychiatric testimony—that it is more likely than not that they meet the civil standard for commitment.

What is that standard? In most American jurisdictions prior to 1960, the standard was that the individual was "in serious need of [mental] treatment." This standard had the virtue of being one that was acceptable to most psychiatrists, for a large part of their everyday practice was determining who needed mental treatment and of what kind. But the standard suffered from a vagueness and concomitant arbitrariness that troubled courts and legislators. Accordingly, beginning in the mid-1960s, it was replaced, in nearly all jurisdictions, by the current standard: that a particular person, by reason of mental problems, "is a danger to himself or others."

What this means, in practice, is that the psychiatrist testifying at a civil commitment hearing must make a prediction about whether the person is likely to engage in violence. But if there is one thing psychiatrists are not very good at, it is predicting future violence. Indeed, in an amicus brief submitted to the Supreme Court in 1980, the American Psychiatric Association reported that its members were frequently no better than laypeople in predicting violence. The "future danger" test, it argued, was therefore not a very useful one.

In subsequent years, psychiatrists and others have tried to develop more refined instruments for predicting danger, but with only limited success. Yet it remains the test, and the law thus forces psychiatrists called to testify at a civil commitment hearing to make the very prediction they have stated officially they cannot make.

Clearly, then, brain science, or what has passed for it, has had a problematic impact on the law, suggesting that proposed interactions should be approached with caution. Which brings us to cognitive neuroscience. It cannot be doubted that cognitive neuroscience has made considerable advances in recent years. This is largely due to the development of functional magnetic resonance imaging (fMRI), commonly called brain scanning, by which, using a giant magnet, a scientist can observe increases and decreases in the flow of (iron-bearing) blood in the brain that appear to correlate with different mental states. In other words, when someone is thinking about mathematics, blood flows to one part of the brain, and when he is thinking about sex, it flows to another part of the brain. Given the law's focus on matters of the mind, it is hardly surprising that some neuroscientists, and not a few law professors, have suggested that neuroscience has much to offer the law.

Judges themselves have expressed similar interest. For example, a few years ago, in connection with preparing, along with Professor Michael S. Gazzaniga (the father of modern cognitive neuroscience) and various other contributors, *A Judge's Guide to Neuroscience*, I did an informal survey of federal judges and found that they had a host of questions about the possible impact of neuroscience on the law, ranging from "What is an fMRI?" to "Does neuroscience give us new insights into criminal responsibility?" and much in between. But when we consider the actual impact of modern neuroscience on the law thus far, the record is mixed.

Most attempts to apply new advances in neuroscience to individual cases either have been rejected by the courts or have proved to be of little value. Consider, for example, the so-called neuroscientific lie detector. While a scientific way to determine if a witness is lying or telling the truth would seemingly be of great value to the legal system, the existing lie-detecting machine, the polygraph—which presupposes that telling an intentional lie is accompanied by increased sweating, a rising pulse rate, and the like—has proved notoriously unreliable and is banned from almost all courts. But relying on the not unreasonable hypothesis that devising an intentional lie involves different brain activities than simply telling the truth, some neuroscientists have hypothesized that certain brain movements correlated with lying might be detected.

The early studies seemed promising. While undergoing brain scans, participants were asked to randomly lie in response to simple questions (for example, "Is the card you are looking at the ace of spades?"), and the brain activity when they lied (as measured by increased blood flow) was greater than, and different from, the brain activity when they told the truth. But there were problems with these studies, both technical and theoretical. For example, while the participants were supposed to remain perfectly still in the brain scanner, even very small (and not easily detected) physical movements led to increased brain activity appearing on the scans, thus confounding the results.

More significantly, these studies did nothing to resolve the question of whether the increased brain activity was the result of lying or was the result of what the participants were actually doing cognitively (i.e., following orders to randomly make up lies). In these and numerous other ways, the studies were far removed from what might be involved in a court witness's lying.

Nevertheless, on the basis of the early studies, two companies were formed to market neuroscientific lie detection to the public, and one of them tried to introduce its evidence in court in two cases. In one such case, in New York state court, the evidence was held inadmissible on the ground that it infringed on the right of the jury to determine credibility. This rationale is not very convincing. Jurors have no special competence to determine the truth: they do it in the same imperfect way that everyday citizens do in everyday life. So if there were truly a well-tested, highly reliable instrument for helping them determine the truth, its results would be as welcome as, say, DNA evidence is today in assisting juries to decide guilt or innocence.

However, in the second case, *United States v. Semrau* (2011), in federal court in Tennessee, the evidence was also held inadmissible, but this time on much more convincing grounds. The case involved a psychologist who owned two businesses that provided government-reimbursed psychological services to nursing home patients, and the charge was that he had manipulated the billing codes so as to overcharge the government by $3 million. His defense was that the mistakes in coding were unintentional. In that regard, defense counsel sought to introduce testimony from the neuroscientist founder of one of the companies marketing neuroscientific lie detection, to the effect that he had placed the defendant in a brain scanner and asked him questions of the form "Did you intend to cheat the government when you coded and billed these services?" According to the expert, the brain scan evidence showed that the defendant was being honest when he answered such questions "No."

The expert conceded that during one of the three sessions when these questions had been put to the defendant, the brain scan results were consistent with lying; but the expert contended that this was the result of the defendant's being "fatigued" in ways he was not at the other two sessions. The judge found, however, that this supposed anomaly was actually indicative of the doubts already expressed in the scientific literature about the validity and reliability of neuroscientific lie detection. Accordingly, he excluded the evidence as unreliable.

As this example suggests, cognitive neuroscience, despite the considerable publicity it has received, is still not able to produce well-tested, reliable procedures for detecting and measuring specific mental states in specific individuals. If the legal system were to embrace such evidence before it was far better developed than it is at present, the same kinds of dire mistakes that occurred in the situations involving eugenics, lobotomies, psychoanalysis, and recovered memories might well again occur.

This is not to say, however, that the considerable advances in neuroscience over the past few decades are without any relevance to the legal system. Even if it is not yet ready to resolve individual cases, some of its more general conclusions may be helpful in making broad policy decisions of consequence to the legal system. Consider, for example, the common observation that adolescents have less control over impulses than adults. Neuroscience helps explain why this occurs. To put it simply, at puberty several parts of the brain rapidly enlarge. This includes the parts associated with impulsive activity and, a bit later, the parts associated with control over impulses. But the connections between these parts only slowly improve (through the neurological process called myelination) to the point where the communication between the enlarged areas can be sufficiently swift to hold in check new impulsive urges of adolescents. On average, this takes more than a year, and the Supreme Court has cited studies of this kind in reaching its conclusions that the death penalty and life imprisonment are unconstitutional when imposed on those below the age of eighteen because of the inadequacy of their impulse control at the time they committed their crimes and the likelihood that this disability will disappear with time.

On the other hand, neuroscience is not yet close to developing a test for determining the precise degree to which impulse control has developed in any given adolescent—so that, for example, a prosecutor could not fairly rely on neuroscience to determine whether any particular adolescent should be prosecuted as an adult or as a juvenile. Again, the point is that neuroscience is at a stage where it may be able to provide helpful insights to the general development of the law, but not much, if anything, in the way of evidence about individuals in particular cases.

Neuroscience may also be helpful to the development of legal policy in dealing with the problem of drug addiction—a problem that consumes much of both state and federal criminal systems. The United States spends billions of dollars each year both punishing and treating drug addicts, but the success rate of even the most sophisticated treatment programs, as measured by the former addicts who do not resume drug use during the program, is rarely better than 50 percent, and considerably lower if measured by relapses after the program is over.

Why is this so, since most addicts want to quit? A considerable amount of neuroscientific research over the past few decades has been addressed to this problem, and while much of the research remains controversial or simply inconclusive, at least some of the results are now generally accepted in the neuroscientific community. These include, for example, the finding that drug addiction actually alters the way the synapses in certain areas of the brain operate (so that an addict has to have his drug just to feel "normal") and also the finding that the cravings associated with drug addiction will over time come to be generated by secondary cues (ranging from the sight of a needle to a return to a party scene).

These findings suggest, first, that simply getting an addict drug-free and over the symptoms of withdrawal is unlikely to be sufficient to prevent re-addiction in many cases and, second, that very long-term programs, including drug testing over many years and training and retraining addicts to avoid the cues that will trigger a relapse, are likely to be more effective than short-term programs.

Long-term programs would be very expensive, though probably not as expensive as the combined cost of incarceration and short-term treatment programs now imposed on some drug-addicted individuals again and again. Nor would such programs work in every case, for once again, the neuroscience says more about the population as a whole than about any given individual. But if nothing else, the neuroscience about the subject does seem to indicate not just that the present approaches are unlikely to be successful overall but also why this is so.

Neuroscience therefore has something to offer the legal system and, given the rapid rate of its current development, may have even more to offer in the future. For now, however, the lessons of the past suggest that, while neuroscientific advances may be a useful aid in evaluating broad policy initiatives, a too-quick acceptance by the legal system of the latest neuroscientific discoveries may be fraught with danger.

7

WHY HIGH-LEVEL EXECUTIVES ARE EXEMPT FROM PROSECUTION

In stark contrast to the mass incarceration of millions of Americans, mostly of color, charged with street crimes and the like, high-level business executives appear increasingly exempt from criminal prosecution, even when they commit very serious frauds. Indeed, federal prosecutions of business executives in general is currently at one of the lowest levels in years. And to give a particularly egregious example of inaction, in the entire decade that followed the Great Recession, which began in 2008, few if any high-level executives were prosecuted for their role in bringing about an economic collapse that left millions of Americans without jobs, without resources, without hope.

Who and what were responsible for the Great Recession? Was it simply a result of negligence, of the kind of inordinate risk-taking commonly called a bubble, of an imprudent but innocent failure to maintain adequate reserves for a rainy day? Or was it the result, at least in major part, of fraudulent practices, of dubious mortgages portrayed as sound risks and packaged into ever more esoteric financial instruments, the fundamental weaknesses of which were intentionally obscured?

If it was the former—if the recession was due, at worst, to a lack of caution—then the criminal law would have no role to play in the aftermath. For in all but a few circumstances (not here relevant), the fierce weapon called criminal prosecution is directed at intentional misconduct, and nothing less. If the Great Recession was in no part the handiwork of intentionally fraudulent practices by high-level executives, then to prosecute such executives criminally would be scapegoating of the most shallow and despicable kind.

But if, by contrast, the Great Recession was in material part the product of intentional fraud, the failure to prosecute those responsible must be judged one of the most egregious failures of the criminal justice system in many years. Indeed, it would stand in striking contrast to the increased success that federal prosecutors had previously had over the prior fifty years or so in bringing to justice even the highest-level figures who orchestrated mammoth frauds.

In the 1970s, in the aftermath of the junk-bond bubble, which in many ways was a precursor to the bubble in mortgage-backed securities that led to the Great Recession, the progenitors of the fraud were all successfully prosecuted, right up to Michael Milken, the so-called junk-bond king, who misled investors into believing that his pools of junk bonds were creditworthy investments. In the 1980s, the savings-and-loan crisis, which the Great Recession also paralleled in some eerie ways, resulted in the successful criminal prosecution of more than eight hundred individuals, including the primary orchestrator, Charles Keating, who was a master in disguising risk through ever more complex transactions. And again, the widespread accounting frauds of the 1990s—vividly illustrated by Enron and WorldCom, where loans were disguised as sales and losses as assets—led directly to the successful prosecution of such previously respected CEOs as Jeffrey Skilling and Bernie Ebbers.

In striking contrast with these past prosecutions, not a single genuinely high-level executive was successfully prosecuted in connection with the Great Recession, and, given that the statute of limitations has expired on all applicable crimes, it is now clear that none will be. It behooves us to ask why and to assess whether this is part of a longer-term and seemingly bipartisan trend to excuse high-level executives from criminal prosecution.

One possibility, already mentioned, is that no fraud was committed. But the stated opinion of those government entities asked to examine the financial crisis is flatly to the contrary. For example, the Financial Crisis Inquiry Commission, in its final report, uses variants of the word "fraud" no fewer than 157 times in describing what led to the crisis, concluding that there was a "systemic breakdown," not just in accountability but also in ethical behavior.

As the commission found, the signs of fraud were everywhere to be seen, with the number of reports of suspected mortgage fraud rising twentyfold between 1996 and 2005 and then doubling again in the next four years. As early as 2004, FBI assistant director Chris Swecker was publicly warning of the pervasive problem of mortgage fraud, driven by the voracious demand for mortgage-backed securities. Similar warnings, many from within the financial community, were disregarded, not because they were viewed as inaccurate, but because, as one high-level banker put it, "a decision was made that 'We're going to have to hold our nose and start buying the stated product if we want to stay in business.'"

More generally, in the aftermath of the meltdown, there was a broad consensus that the crisis was in material respects the product of intentional fraud. And, as many government officials noted (albeit with the benefit of hindsight), the fraud was a simple one. Subprime mortgages (i.e., mortgages of dubious creditworthiness and, in too many cases, disguised to conceal their weakness) increasingly provided the chief collateral for highly leveraged securities that were marketed as A, AA, or even AAA securities of very low risk. How could this transformation of a sow's ear into a silk purse be accomplished unless someone dissembled along the way?

While officials at the Department of Justice were initially more circumspect in attributing the roots of the financial crisis to fraud, eventually they, too, agreed with this analysis—as shown, for example, by the charges of civil fraud they brought in my own court, and elsewhere, against some of the major banks. But they never went after the banking and other executives who oversaw these frauds. They excused their failure to do so on one or more of three grounds.

First, they argued that establishing fraudulent intent on the part of the managers of the banks and companies involved in such massive frauds was too difficult to prove. It is undoubtedly true that the ranks of top management were several levels removed from those who were putting together the collateralized debt obligations and other securities offerings that were based on dubious mortgages. It's also true that the people generating the mortgages themselves were often at other companies and thus even further removed.

But as former chief of business fraud prosecutions in the Manhattan U.S. Attorney's Office, I found it surprising that the DOJ should view the proving of fraudulent intent by high-level executives as so difficult in these cases when the same objection had been repeatedly rejected, and overcome, in such equally complex cases as Enron and WorldCom. Who, for example, was generating the so-called suspicious activity reports of mortgage fraud that, as mentioned, increased so hugely in the years leading up to the crisis? Why, the banks themselves. A top-level banker, one might argue, confronted with growing evidence from his own and other banks that mortgage fraud was increasing, might have inquired why his bank's mortgage-based securities continued to receive AAA ratings. And if, despite these and other reports of suspicious activity, the executive failed to make such inquiries, might it be because he did not want to know what they would reveal?

This is what is known in the law as "willful blindness" or "conscious disregard." It is a well-established basis on which federal prosecutors have asked juries to infer a high-level executive's knowledge of fraud, including in cases involving complexities, such as accounting rules, at least as esoteric as those involved in the events leading up to the financial crisis. And while some federal courts have occasionally expressed qualifications about the use of the willful blindness approach to prove intent, the Supreme Court has consistently approved it. As that Court stated most recently in *Global-Tech Appliances, Inc. v. SEB S.A.* (2011):

> The doctrine of willful blindness is well established in criminal law. Many criminal statutes require proof that a defendant acted knowingly or willfully, and courts applying the doctrine of willful blindness hold that defendants cannot escape the reach of these statutes by deliberately shielding themselves from clear evidence of critical facts that are strongly suggested by the circumstances.

Thus, the DOJ's claim that proving intent on the part of high-level executives supervising the fraudulent activities that preceded the financial crisis was particularly difficult may strike some as doubtful.

Second, and even weaker, the DOJ sometimes argued that, because the institutions to whom mortgage-backed securities were sold were themselves sophisticated investors, it might be difficult to prove that they reasonably relied on the fraudulent misrepresentations (as opposed to simply accepting the risk in order to foist the securities onto third parties). Thus, in defending the failure to prosecute high-level executives for frauds arising from the sale of mortgage-backed securities, Lanny Breuer, the head of the DOJ's Criminal Division, told PBS in 2013:

> In a criminal case . . . I have to prove not only that you made a false statement but that you intended to commit a crime, and also that the other side of the transaction relied on what you were saying. And frankly, in many of the securitizations and the kinds of transactions we're talking about, in reality you had very sophisticated counterparties on both sides. And so even though one side may have said something was dark blue when really we can say it was sky blue, the other side of the transaction, the other sophisticated party, wasn't relying at all on the description of the color.

Actually, given the fact that these securities were bought and sold at lightning speed, it is by no means obvious that even a sophisticated counterparty would have detected the problems with the arcane, convoluted mortgage-backed derivatives they were being asked to purchase and were being assured were sound and suitable. But there is a more fundamental problem with the above-quoted statement from the head of the Criminal Division, which is that it totally misstates the law. In actuality, in a criminal fraud case the government is never required to prove—ever—

that one party to a transaction relied on the word of another. The reason, of course, is that that would give a crooked seller a license to lie whenever he was dealing with a buyer, whether sophisticated or careless, who might have made the purchase for unrelated reasons. The criminal law, however, says that society is harmed when a seller purposely lies about a material fact, even if the immediate purchaser does not rely on that particular fact, because such misrepresentations create problems for the market as a whole. And surely there never was a situation in which the sale of dubious mortgage-backed securities created more of a problem for the marketplace, and society as a whole, than in the recent financial crisis.

The third reason the department sometimes gave for not bringing these prosecutions was that to do so would itself harm the economy. In 2009, Attorney General Eric Holder told Congress: "It does become difficult for us to prosecute them when we are hit with indications that if you do prosecute—if you do bring a criminal charge—it will have a negative impact on the national economy, perhaps even the world economy."

To a federal judge, who takes an oath to apply the law equally to rich and to poor, this excuse—sometimes labeled the "too big to jail" excuse—is disturbing, frankly, in what it says about the DOJ's apparent disregard for equality under the law. Holder himself, while he could not deny what he had said, later claimed it had been misconstrued. But even on its face, his comment is no excuse for not prosecuting high-level executives. For while, theoretically, it might harm the economy to prosecute a large bank or corporation (though even this is doubtful), no one can seriously claim that simply going after individuals would somehow materially impact the economy as a whole.

Perhaps Holder might have also been influenced, as his department unquestionably was, by the adverse reaction to the case of Arthur Andersen, the accounting firm forced out of business by a prosecution that was ultimately reversed on appeal. But, again, if we are talking about prosecuting individuals, the excuse becomes entirely irrelevant, for no one that I know of has ever contended that a big financial institution would collapse if one or more of its high-level executives were prosecuted, as opposed to the institution itself.

These dubious arguments illustrate that the officials of the DOJ never took the position that all the top executives involved in the events leading up to the financial crisis were innocent. Rather, they offered one or another excuse for not criminally prosecuting them—excuses that, on inspection, appear entirely unconvincing. So, you might ask, what's really going on here?

Some people have inferred that no such prosecutions were brought because the top prosecutors were often people who previously represented the financial institutions in question and/or were people who expected to be representing such institutions in the future: the so-called revolving door excuse. While this may be a problem with many regulatory agencies, I am inclined to discount it when it comes to the DOJ, at least below the very top levels. In my experience, most line prosecutors are seeking to make a name for themselves, and the best way to do that is by prosecuting some high-level person. While companies that are indicted almost always settle, individual defendants whose careers are at stake will sometimes go to trial. And if the government wins such a trial, as it usually does, the prosecutor's reputation is made.

To be sure, some administrations are more forgiving of big business than others. And top-level prosecutors who have previously represented high-level executives may be more "understanding" of the difficulties top management faces in getting a handle on misconduct. My point is that whatever small influence the revolving door may have in discouraging certain white-collar prosecutions is more than offset, at least in the case of prosecuting high-level individuals, by the career-making benefits such prosecutions confer on the successful prosecutor, as well as on his chief.

So, one asks again, why didn't we see such prosecutions following the financial crisis? I offer, by way of speculation, three influences that I think, along with others, had the effect of limiting such prosecutions.

First, the prosecutors had other priorities. Some of these were completely understandable. For example, before 2001, the FBI had more than one thousand agents assigned to investigating financial fraud, but after the September 11 attacks many of these agents were shifted to antiterrorism work. Who can argue with that? Yet the result was that, by 2007 or so, there were only 120 agents reviewing the more than fifty thousand reports of mortgage fraud filed by the banks. It is true that after the collapse of Lehman Brothers in 2008, new agents were hired for some of the vacated spots in offices concerned with fraud detection; but this is not a form of detection easily learned, and subsequent budget limitations only exacerbated the problem.

However, while the FBI has substantial responsibility for investigating mortgage fraud, the FBI is not the primary investigator of fraud in the sale of mortgage-backed securities; that responsibility lies mostly with the U.S. Securities and Exchange Commission (SEC). But at the very time the financial crisis was breaking, the SEC was trying to deflect criticism from its failure to detect the fraud perpetrated by Bernard Madoff, and this led it to concentrate on other Ponzi-like schemes that emerged after the financial crisis, along with cases involving misallocation of assets (such as stealing funds from a customer), which are among the easiest cases to prove. Indeed, as Professor John Coffee of Columbia Law School has repeatedly documented, Ponzi schemes and misallocation-of-asset cases have been the primary focus of the SEC since 2009. More generally, because of budget constraints, the SEC has increasingly focused on its batting average, in order to convince the members of Congress concerned with the SEC's budget that the agency has been highly successful in the cases it has brought. While a successful case against a high-level executive can be beneficial to the SEC's image, putting together at the outset the kind of large team necessary to make such a case, without any guarantee that the case will be made, is far more problematic.

As for the DOJ proper, a decision was made in 2009 to spread the investigation of financial fraud cases among numerous U.S. Attorney's Offices, many of which had little or no previous experience in investigating and prosecuting sophisticated financial frauds. This was in connection with the president's creation of a special task force to investigate the crisis, from which remarkably little was ever heard in subsequent years. At the same time, the U.S. Attorney's Office with the greatest expertise in these kinds of cases, the Southern District of New York, was just embarking on its prosecution of insider-trading cases arising from the Raj Rajaratnam tapes, which soon proved a gold mine of prosecutable cases that absorbed a huge amount of the attention of the securities fraud unit of that office.

While I have no inside information, as a former chief of that unit I would venture to guess that the cases involving the financial crisis were parceled out to assistant U.S. attorneys who were also responsible for insider-trading cases. Which do you think an assistant would devote most of her attention to: an insider-trading case that was nearly ready to go to indictment and that might lead to a high-visibility trial, or a financial crisis case that was just getting started, would take years to complete, and had no guarantee of even leading to an indictment? It seems more than likely that she would put her energy into the insider-trading case, and if she was lucky, it would go to trial, she would win, and, in many cases, she would then take a job with a large law firm. And in the process, the financial fraud case would get lost in the shuffle.

In short, a focus on quite different priorities is, I submit, one of the reasons that financial fraud cases against high-level individuals were not brought in the wake of the Great Recession, or since then, especially since such cases take many years, many investigators, and a great deal of expertise to investigate, with no assurance of success.

But a second, and less salutary, reason why such cases were not brought was the government's own involvement in the underlying circumstances that led to the financial crisis. Indeed, the government, writ large, played a significant part in creating the conditions that encouraged the approval of dubious mortgages. Even before the start of the housing boom, it was the government, in the form of Congress, that repealed the Glass-Steagall Act, which had barred banks from securities trading. Prior to the repeal, banks had viewed mortgages as a source of long-term interest income, and so they were cautious in giving out mortgage loans. But after the repeal, banks shifted their focus and became deeply involved in securitizing pools of mortgages in order to obtain the much greater profits available from trading interests in these pools. They therefore had much less incentive to exercise close supervision over the soundness of the underlying mortgages, relying instead on third-party mortgage brokers to supply them with sufficient new mortgages to create new pools. It was the government, by repealing Glass-Steagall, that created this change in priorities.

It was also the government, in the form of both the executive and the legislature, that encouraged banking deregulation, thus weakening the power and oversight not only of the SEC but also of such diverse banking overseers as the Office of Thrift Supervision and the Office of the Comptroller of the Currency, both in the Treasury Department. It was the government, in the form of the Federal Reserve, that kept interest rates low, in part to encourage mortgages. It was the government, in the form of the executive, that strongly encouraged banks to make loans to individuals with low incomes who might have previously been regarded as too risky to warrant a mortgage. Thus, in the year 2000, HUD secretary Andrew Cuomo increased to 50 percent the percentage of low-income mortgages that the government-sponsored entities known as Fannie Mae and Freddie Mac were required to purchase, helping to create the conditions that resulted in over half of all mortgages being subprime at the time the housing market began to collapse in 2007.

It was also the government, pretty much across the board, that acquiesced in the ever-greater tendency not to require meaningful documentation as a condition of obtaining a mortgage, often preempting in this regard state regulations designed to assure greater mortgage quality and a borrower's ability to repay. Indeed, in the year 2000, the Office of Thrift Supervision, having just finished a successful campaign to preempt state regulation of thrift underwriting, terminated its own underwriting regulations entirely.

The results of all this were the mortgages that later became known as "liars' loans." They were increasingly risky, but what did the banks care, since they were making their money from the securitizations? And what did the government care, since it was helping to create a boom in the economy and helping voters to realize their dream of owning a home?

Moreover, the government was also deeply enmeshed in the aftermath of the financial crisis. It was the government that proposed the shotgun marriages of, among others, Bank of America with Merrill Lynch, and of J.P. Morgan with Bear Stearns. If, in the process, mistakes were made and liabilities not disclosed, was it not partly the government's fault? One does not necessarily have to adopt the view of Neil Barofsky, former special inspector general in charge of oversight of the government's Troubled Asset Relief Program (TARP), that regulators made almost no effort to hold accountable the financial institutions they were bailing out, to wonder whether the government, having helped create the conditions that led to the seeming widespread fraud in the mortgage-backed securities market, was all too ready to forgive its alleged perpetrators.

Please do not misunderstand me. I am not suggesting that the government knowingly participated in any of the fraudulent practices alleged by the Financial Inquiry Crisis Commission and others. But what I am suggesting is that the government was deeply involved, from beginning to end, in helping create the conditions that could lead to such fraud, and that this would give a prudent prosecutor pause in deciding whether to indict a CEO who might, with some justice, claim that he was only doing what he fairly believed the government wanted him to do.

One also wonders whether, given the current strong push of the Trump administration for across-the-board deregulation (not least of banks), the government might well be in the process of re-creating the conditions in which financial fraud can flourish.

The final factor I would mention is both the most subtle and the most systemic of the three, and the most important. It is the shift that has occurred, over the past twenty years or more, from focusing on prosecuting high-level individuals to focusing on prosecuting companies and financial institutions. It is true that prosecutors have brought criminal charges against companies for well over a hundred years, but until relatively recently, such prosecutions were the exception, and prosecutions of companies without simultaneous prosecutions of their managerial agents were even rarer.

The reasons were obvious. Companies do not commit crimes; only their agents do. And while a company might get the benefit of some such crimes, prosecuting the company would inevitably punish, directly or indirectly, the many employees and shareholders who were totally innocent. Moreover, under the law of most U.S. jurisdictions, a company cannot be criminally liable unless at least one managerial agent has committed the crime in question, so why not prosecute the agent who actually committed the crime?

In recent decades, however, prosecutors have been increasingly attracted to prosecuting companies, often even without indicting a single person. This shift has been rationalized as part of an attempt to transform corporate cultures, so as to prevent such crimes in the future. As a result, government policy has taken the form of "deferred prosecution agreements" or even "non-prosecution agreements," in which the company, under threat of criminal prosecution, agrees to take various prophylactic measures to prevent future wrongdoing. Such agreements have become, in the words of Lanny Breuer, the previously mentioned former head of the DOJ's Criminal Division, "a mainstay of white-collar criminal law enforcement," with the department entering into more than 250 such agreements over the past fifteen years. But in practice, I suggest, this approach has led to some lax and dubious behavior on the part of prosecutors, with deleterious results.

If you are a prosecutor attempting to discover the individuals responsible for an apparent financial fraud, you go about your business in much the same way you go after mobsters or drug kingpins: you start at the bottom and, over many months or years, slowly work your way up. Specifically, you start by "flipping" some low- or mid-level participant in the fraud who, you can show, was directly responsible for making one or more false material misrepresentations but who is willing to cooperate, and maybe even wear a wire (i.e., secretly record his colleagues) in order to reduce his sentence. With his help, and aided by the substantial prison penalties now available in white-collar cases, you go up the ladder.

But if your priority is prosecuting the company, a different scenario takes place. Early in the investigation, you invite in counsel to the company and explain to her why you suspect fraud. She responds by assuring you that the company wants to cooperate and do the right thing, and to that end the company has hired a former federal prosecutor, now a partner at a respected law firm, to do an internal investigation. The company's counsel asks you to defer your investigation until the company's own internal investigation is completed, on the condition that the company will share its results with you. In order to save time and resources, you agree.

Six months later the company's counsel returns, with a detailed report showing that mistakes were made but that the company is now intent on correcting them. You and the company then agree that the company will enter into a deferred prosecution agreement that couples some immediate fines with the imposition of expensive but internal prophylactic measures. For all practical purposes the case is now over. You are happy because you believe that you have helped prevent future crimes; the company is happy because it has avoided a devastating indictment; and perhaps the happiest of all are the executives, or former executives, who actually committed the underlying misconduct, for they are left untouched.

Following the financial crisis, such approaches became endemic. Increasingly large fines, coupled to expensive compliance programs, were imposed on banks and other financial institutions; but the human beings who committed the actual frauds or, even worse, oversaw their commission were left alone. This trend has continued regardless of the administration, so that, as noted, federal prosecution of business executives in general is now at the lowest level it has been in many decades.

I suggest that this is not the best way to proceed. Although going after the company is supposedly justified because it prevents future crimes, I suggest that the future deterrent value of successfully prosecuting individuals far outweighs the prophylactic benefits of imposing internal compliance measures that are often little more than window-dressing. And even large fines rarely approach the amount of profits realized from the fraud, and thus become simply a cost of doing business.

Nor is this just my opinion. In 2014, Professor Brandon Garrett (now at Duke Law School) published, under the title *Too Big to Jail*, what is generally considered to be the definitive study of all federal corporate criminal prosecution agreements (including nonprosecution and deferred prosecution agreements) since 1996. As I will discuss in chapter 8, Garrett concluded that there was a high rate of recidivism, with some major banks and corporations breaking one deferred prosecution agreement after another— only to be further "punished" by increased fines and compliance measures, but no prosecution of high-level individuals.

Just going after the company is also both technically and morally suspect. It is technically suspect because, under the law, you should not indict or threaten to indict a company unless you can prove beyond a reasonable doubt that some managerial agent of the company committed the alleged crime; and if you can prove that, why not indict the manager? And from a moral standpoint, punishing a company and its many innocent employees and shareholders for the crimes committed by some unprosecuted individuals seems contrary to elementary notions of moral responsibility.

Such criticisms by numerous observers (most prominently, Senator Elizabeth Warren) eventually led to sufficient public outcry that, toward the end of the Obama administration, Deputy Attorney General Sally Yates issued what was called the Yates Memorandum, directing a greater focus on prosecuting individuals and not just companies. But by this time, the statute of limitations had run out on most charges of fraud arising from the financial crisis, so the memorandum was really more of a suggestion as to how to handle other, future frauds. Shortly thereafter, moreover, Yates was fired by the new president, Donald Trump, and the current DOJ has shown little appetite for going after high-level individuals, unless they happen to be executives of foreign companies.

In hindsight, the financial crisis that brought so much economic and social misery to so many innocent people increasingly appears to have been the product of fraudulent misconduct. The intentional failure of the government to bring to justice those responsible for such colossal fraud bespeaks weaknesses in our prosecutorial system that could be easily fixed by returning to the prosecution of responsible high-level executives, as occurred regularly in the period from roughly 1965 to 1995. It is hard to avoid the conclusion that our otherwise very aggressive criminal justice system gives a pass to those who can take advantage of a corporate shield.

8

JUSTICE DEFERRED IS JUSTICE DENIED

As discussed in chapter 7, the DOJ has increasingly responded to high-level corporate crime not by prosecuting the individuals who actually committed the crimes, but by entering into deferred prosecution agreements with the companies that benefited from the crimes. While a case might be made for doing both—that is, both prosecuting the individuals and entering into prophylactic agreements with their companies—in practice the latter has pretty much superseded the former. It is therefore worth taking a closer look at corporate criminal deferred prosecution agreements, to see what they accomplish, if anything.

So-called deferred prosecutions were developed in the 1930s as a way of helping juvenile offenders. A juvenile who had been charged with a crime would agree with the prosecutor to have his prosecution deferred while he entered a program designed to rehabilitate such offenders. If he successfully completed the program and committed no other crime over the course of a year, the charge would then be dropped.

The analogy of a Fortune 500 company to a juvenile delinquent is, perhaps, less than obvious. Nonetheless, beginning in the early 1990s and with increasing frequency thereafter, federal prosecutors began entering into deferred prosecution agreements with major corporations and large financial institutions. In the typical arrangement, the government agreed to defer prosecuting the company for various federal felonies if the company, in addition to paying a financial penalty, agreed to introduce various prophylactic measures designed to prevent future such crimes and to rehabilitate the company's culture. The crimes for which prosecution was thus deferred included felony violations of the securities laws, banking laws, antitrust laws, anti–money laundering laws, food and drug laws, foreign corrupt practices laws, and numerous provisions of the general federal criminal code.

The intellectual origins of this approach to corporate crime can be traced back at least to the 1980s, when various academics suggested that the best way to deter "crime in the suites" was to foster a culture within companies of acting ethically and responsibly. In practice, this meant encouraging companies not only to provide in-house ethical training but also to enlarge their internal compliance programs, so that responsible behavior would be praised and misconduct policed. The approach found favor not just with some corporations (notably General Electric under the guidance of its general counsel, Ben Heineman), but also with the U.S. Sentencing Commission, which, in promulgating the corporate sentencing guidelines in 1991, made the overall adequacy of a company's prior internal compliance programs the most important factor in reducing (by as much as 60 percent) the size of the fine to be imposed on a company found guilty of a federal criminal violation.

The DOJ then went a step further and, in a series of memoranda issued over the succeeding two decades, made the existence or absence of a meaningful internal compliance program an important consideration in determining whether or not to prosecute a company for crimes committed by its employees—the theory being that, if a company had a good compliance program already in place, its employees' crimes were aberrational and not reflective of corporate irresponsibility, whereas the absence of a good compliance program indicated a lax corporate attitude toward crime.

But the department did not stop there. In the same memoranda (including the Thompson Memorandum, the McCallum Memorandum, and the McNulty Memorandum, all named after the various deputy attorney generals in charge), the department stated that another important factor to be considered in deciding whether to criminally charge a company was any effort taken after the crime was uncovered "to implement an effective corporate compliance program or to improve an existing one." This led counsel for companies that were otherwise unsuccessful in avoiding prosecution to argue, with ever greater success, that the best response to their alleged misconduct was not to punish them (and their innocent shareholders and employees) but to rehabilitate them by deferring prosecution while they instituted a more rigorous compliance program, upon the successful completion of which the charges would be dropped.

It took a while for this to catch on, but in recent years deferred prosecution agreements have become commonplace, so that, in the decade between 2008 and 2018, the DOJ entered into more than 250 such agreements (including so-called non-prosecution agreements, i.e., deferred prosecution agreements that were not even presented to a court for approval) with major companies and financial institutions. And the trend has continued into the current administration. Thus, for example, in 2020, the DOJ entered into a deferred prosecution with Wells Fargo Bank as a result of its massive creation of phony bank accounts.

The three common features of most (though not all) of these agreements were the payment of a fine, the introduction of ethical training for employees, and the implementation of new or improved compliance programs, usually described in general terms such as "effective compliance" or "appropriate due diligence." Going one step further, these three features increasingly became the hallmark of the written plea agreements that the department reached with even those companies that did not receive a deferred prosecution but instead agreed to plead guilty outright.

As mentioned in chapter 7, Professor Brandon Garrett, in his 2014 book *Too Big to Jail*, provided a detailed and comprehensive examination of deferred corporate prosecutions entered into up to that time, as well as corporate criminal prosecutions generally, and concluded that they had been, on the whole, ineffective. According to Garrett, "the big story of the twenty-first century" in corporate prosecutions is that "prosecutors now try to rehabilitate a company by helping it to put systems in place to detect and prevent crime among its employees and, more broadly, to foster a culture of ethics and integrity inside the company." But Garrett—on the basis of his own painstaking gathering of evidence (for neither the DOJ nor any other governmental entity keeps detailed and complete records of how such agreements are implemented over time)—concludes that many, and perhaps most, such agreements, fail to achieve meaningful structural or ethical reform within the company itself. At the same time, such agreements tend to obscure the identities of the people who were actually responsible for the company's misconduct.

To help explain these failures, it may be useful to examine

some of the premises that underlie corporate criminal prosecutions and deferred prosecution agreements.

To begin with, there is the assumption that criminal prosecution of corporations makes sense as a general matter. This is far from obvious. As Garrett points out in passing, "few foreign countries have anything like the broad standard for corporate criminal liability that the United States has long had in federal courts." One might ask why this is so. Ultimately, it rests on the recognition by these other countries that companies can act only through their employees, and therefore, as most of these countries believe, it is more appropriate to prosecute the responsible employees than the entity that employed them.

Relatedly, criminal prosecution of corporations inevitably engenders collateral consequences that often seem at odds with the purposes of the criminal law. Since a corporation cannot be put in jail, the primary penalty is usually a fine, and since a criminal fine is usually not covered by insurance, the cost of the fine comes out of the corporate treasury and so is ultimately borne by the company's shareholders, who generally had nothing to do with the underlying criminal activity. In addition, the greater the monetary penalty, the more likely the company will have to discharge many likewise innocent employees, not to mention trying (if the market will allow) to pass on the costs to innocent consumers through increased prices. Why should the criminal law be used to punish the innocent?

It might be argued that even innocent shareholders are often beneficiaries of the misconduct, for example, when their shares increase in value as a result of a corporate fraud. But their shares will typically fall when the fraud is exposed; and even when that is not the case, the company will usually be sued civilly, thus further reducing any benefit the shareholders might derive from the fraud. As for the argument that prosecuting the company will lead the shareholders to demand new management, in my experience over the last nearly fifty years as a white-collar prosecutor, defense lawyer, and judge, this has rarely been the case, except when the managers are themselves prosecuted.

There may be cases in which, in addition to prosecuting the responsible individuals, it makes sense to prosecute the company because (as in the case of some family-owned or closely held companies) the company was no more than a cover for the fraud and deserves to be dissolved. One might even argue (though I would not) that prosecution of a company is warranted when the crime was committed for the benefit of the company by its high managerial agents, who are also being prosecuted. This possibility is recognized by the state laws of most of the fifty states, which restrict the criminal prosecution of companies to cases in which, in the words of the Model Penal Code adopted by many of these states, "the commission of the offense was authorized, requested, commanded, performed or recklessly tolerated by the board of directors or by a high managerial agent acting in behalf of the corporation within the scope of his office or employment."

But the federal law of corporate criminal liability is far more sweeping. Under federal law, corporations can be held criminally liable if even a low-level employee, in the course of his or her employment, commits a criminal act that benefits the corporation. One might think, therefore, that federal corporate prosecutions, whether deferred or otherwise, would typically be accompanied by prosecution of the responsible individuals. But more often than not, this has not been the case, especially when large companies are involved. Rather, in recent years the federal government has brought many corporate prosecutions in which no employee has been prosecuted or even identified as criminally responsible.

This is especially true in the case of deferred prosecutions. According to Garrett, "in about two-thirds of the cases involving deferred prosecution or non-prosecution agreements and public corporations, the company was punished but no employees were prosecuted." This suggests that the DOJ has been persuaded by its own rhetoric that the main point of these agreements is to change corporate culture, so that company employees at all levels will be dissuaded in the future from committing company-related crimes.

But this raises a host of questions, including what is meant by "corporate culture," how it can be altered, and, if it can, whether deferred prosecutions can do the trick. Garrett largely focuses on the latter question, arguing that most corporate prosecution agreements are not adequately enforced and that, perhaps as a result, there is much recidivism on the part of the companies. But we first need to be clear on what we mean by "corporate culture" and what we know, if anything, about how it can be changed.

The term "corporate culture" is quite vague, and the sociological studies about it are inconsistent and often wrapped in impenetrable jargon. No major company fails to tell its employees that irresponsible conduct will not be tolerated, and very few lack a substantial compliance program. What, then, is the basis for the assumption—at the heart of the corporate sentencing guidelines and of almost all deferred prosecution agreements—that even though a substantial compliance program failed to prevent the wrongdoing at issue, an even more costly program will do so in the future?

Speaking of corporate culture in an even broader way, it is worth remembering that any reasonable shareholder wants his or her company's executives to be characterized by energy, initiative, competitiveness, innovativeness, and even aggressiveness, all in a quest for profitability. But these lauded qualities, essential to success in any competitive company, may in some cases encourage questionable behavior. For example, Enron, before the exposure of its fraud, was for six consecutive years named by *Fortune* magazine as one of America's "most admired" companies, mainly because of its highly innovative business practices. Unfortunately, such "innovation" extended to structuring its transactions in ways that made them appear far more profitable than they actually were. But does that mean that we want to use the criminal law to discourage innovation per se?

At bottom, corporate fraud amounts to little more than executives lying for business purposes, and prosecution depends on proving that the lies were intentional. Are the changes forced upon companies by deferred prosecution agreements—chiefly, more ethical training programs and greater oversight by more compliance officers—likely to materially change the decision of these individuals to lie when it suits their goals? The theory of the federal corporate sentencing guidelines and most deferred prosecution agreements is that they will; but the data thus far fail to support this claim (assuming, which itself may be doubtful, that it can ever really be measured).

Take the case of the huge pharmaceutical company Pfizer Inc. In 2002, Pfizer—having been threatened with prosecution for one of its subsidiaries' paying large bribes to a managed care company to give preferred status to one of Pfizer's drugs—entered into a deferred prosecution agreement that, among other things, required it to create and implement a compliance mechanism that would uncover illegal marketing activities and bring them to the attention of its board. None of the employees who paid the bribes, approved their payment, or concealed their true purpose was prosecuted.

Two years later, however, the company was again facing prosecution for similar illegal marketing activities that had continued at the same subsidiary. Still, no individuals were prosecuted. Instead, the subsidiary entered a corporate plea, and Pfizer itself entered into a second deferred prosecution agreement that required even more extensive steps to uncover illegal activities, stop them from being carried out, and bring them to the attention of its board.

Yet notwithstanding this second agreement, in 2007 still further criminal marketing activities by another of Pfizer's subsidiaries—which had illegally promoted off-label marketing of a human growth hormone with dangerous side effects—led to another corporate guilty plea by the subsidiary and still another agreement by Pfizer to increase its requirements that its employees comply with the law. Once again, no individuals were prosecuted.

Despite these three consecutive deferred prosecution agreements requiring enhanced compliance, in 2009 Pfizer, the parent company, was detected engaging in the same lucrative but flagrantly illegal marketing activities, including bribes to doctors to promote off-label uses of Pfizer's drugs, bribes to medical journals to publish articles promoting such uses, and much more. And how did the DOJ deal with the fact that, despite all the prior deferred prosecution agreements and promises of enhanced compliance, the same illegal marketing activities had now come to pervade the parent corporation itself?

The government did not prosecute the senior executives who were alleged to have known of, in some cases orchestrated, and in other cases covered up these illegal activities. Instead, the DOJ entered into still another deferred prosecution agreement with Pfizer by which it paid penalties of $2.3 billion—which the government trumpeted as the largest criminal fine ever imposed to that date, but which analysts suggested was a small fraction of the profits derived from the illegal activity—and by requiring still further compliance improvements. As the DOJ stated in announcing this "historic" settlement: "Pfizer has agreed to enter into an expansive corporate integrity agreement . . . [that] provides for procedures and reviews to be put in place to avoid and promptly detect conduct similar to that which gave rise to this matter." In view of Pfizer's record, this seemed an astonishing act of faith. And, indeed, in 2012, Pfizer was found to have committed still further crimes—this time, illegal foreign bribes—and entered into yet another deferred prosecution agreement.

Pfizer may be the extreme case, but Garrett's book shows pretty definitively that many, and perhaps most, companies that enter into deferred prosecution agreements sooner or later commit new crimes. So why do prosecutors continue to be enamored of deferred prosecution agreements? Partly, of course, it is to conserve resources; because of the reach of federal law, as discussed above, prosecuting a company is far easier, and requires far less investigation, than going after high-level executives of the company. Also, by deferring actual prosecution, a deferred prosecution agreement avoids the unfair collateral consequences noted above. Pfizer, for example, would have been banned from selling prescription drugs if it had actually entered a guilty plea, thus quite possibly forcing it out of business; and the deleterious impact would have been primarily borne not by the executives responsible for the misdeeds, but by the innocent shareholders and employees.

The department's preference for deferred prosecutions also reflects some questionable motives, such as the political advantages of a settlement that makes for a good press release; the avoidance of unpredictable courtroom battles with skilled, highly paid adversaries; and even the dubious benefit to the DOJ and the defendant of crafting a settlement that limits, or eliminates entirely, judicial oversight of implementation of the agreement.

The bottom line is that, for the past two decades or more, as a result of the shift from prosecuting high-level individuals to entering into cosmetic prosecution agreements with their companies, the punishment and deterrence of corporate crime has, for all the government's rhetoric, effectively been reduced. And, even worse, the persons who actually committed these substantial crimes have gone entirely unprosecuted.

9

THE SHRINKAGE OF LEGAL OVERSIGHT

The problems with our criminal legal system discussed in the preceding chapters are the result, among other causes, of a diminishment in the power of the courts, and especially the federal courts, to make sure the system works fairly. Thus, for example, a large contributor to the problem of mass incarceration has been mandatory minimum sentences, by which Congress and state legislatures take much of the sentencing power away from judges (who, in most cases, tend to be lenient) and decree that the judges must impose minimum sentences that are frequently harsh. But so, too, everything from the pressures put on innocent street criminals to plead guilty to crimes they never committed to the increasing tendency of prosecutors to substitute deferred prosecutions of corporations for actual prosecution of high-level executives is greatly aided by the fact that judges have been given only limited oversight of plea bargains of any kind.

This extends as well to civil settlements between private companies and government regulatory authorities. Thus, when, in 2012, I refused to approve a patently inadequate $285 million settlement between the SEC and Citigroup arising from the latter's dumping on misled investors billions of dollars of worthless mortgage-backed securities, the Court of Appeals reversed my decision, proclaiming that courts had no role to play whatsoever in evaluating such settlements.

In some ways, however, the most insidious reduction in the role of the federal courts in overseeing how the system operates has been the diminishment in its power to utilize the writ of habeas corpus to review what goes on in both the state and federal systems of criminal justice. The writ is, technically, an order from a federal court requiring the government (state or federal) to bring an imprisoned person before the court so that the court can determine whether the person was imprisoned fairly and in accordance with fundamental legal principles. But in recent decades, this power has been severely diminished. To appreciate just how disturbing this change has been, it is necessary to briefly examine the history of the writ and similar protections, going back to the time of the famous document known as the Magna Carta.

The Magna Carta, which dates to 1215, is one of the most celebrated, and least read, of the world's legal texts. The great twentieth-century British jurist Lord Denning described the Magna Carta as "the greatest constitutional document of all times—the foundation of the freedom of the individual against the arbitrary authority of the despot." But it was not always held in such high repute. Pope Innocent III, in annulling the Magna Carta just a couple of months after it was promulgated (though it was later reinstated), declared that the charter was "not only shameful and demeaning but also illegal and unjust." And as a peace treaty between King John and certain rebel barons—which was its purpose—the Magna Carta was something of a flop, with the rebellion continuing even after John's death in 1216.

The Magna Carta was reputedly drafted by Stephen Langton, the archbishop of Canterbury, and while his authorship has been called into question regarding the overall document, it seems likely he was responsible for the very first operative clause, or chapter. That chapter affirms that "the English Church shall be free, and shall have its rights undiminished, and its liberties unimpaired." However, while chapter 1 might be read as a statement of religious freedom, this does not appear to have been the chief concern of the barons who negotiated the charter: for what follows, in chapters 2–8, is a series of protections for the barons' widows and heirs against attempts by King John to seize the barons' lands and properties upon their deaths. Given the modest life expectancy of the average English baron in those days, it was probably these provisions that were uppermost in the barons' minds.

But what if the baron died while still indebted to those medieval moneylenders, the Jews? Chapters 10 and 11 provide protection for a baron's wife and children against having to pay interest for a time on debts owed to Jews, who are expressly singled out in this regard. It is remarkable, and disappointing, that so little attention has been paid by subsequent commentators to these anti-Semitic, discriminatory, and rather cavalierly derogatory chapters. In fairness, however, the real purpose of these clauses was, as indicated, to prevent a baron's property from falling into the hands of the king after the baron's death. This was because Jews in medieval England were forbidden to own property. Indeed, Jews themselves were considered to be a form of property: chattels belonging to the king. Thus, if a baron or his heirs defaulted on a debt by not paying interest, the property securing the debt became the property of the king.

For this reason, John viewed the Jews as useful tools (unlike John's famous predecessor Richard the Lionheart, who went out of his way to encourage their murder); and thus these chapters of the Magna Carta may even be viewed as providing a certain legal validation, not otherwise always provided, of debts owed to Jews. But even if read generously in this way, these provisions hardly presaged a greater acceptance of Jews by either the barons or the Crown. Seventy-five years later, in 1290, King Edward I issued an order expelling all Jews from England.

The next twenty-five chapters or so are chiefly concerned with taxes, fines, and other assessments by the Crown, and are not without relevance to future laws forbidding excessive fines and the like, or even, in chapter 12's prohibition of scutage (a tax levied in lieu of military service) without consent, the doctrine of no taxation without representation. But it is only when we get to chapter 39 that we find the language for which the Magna Carta is chiefly known: "No free man shall be seized or imprisoned, or stripped of his rights or possessions, or outlawed or exiled, or deprived of his standing in any other way, nor will we proceed with force against him, or send others to do so, except by the lawful judgement of his equals or by the law of the land."

Much of what we would today refer to as the right to due process and, more broadly, the rule of law is neatly summed up in this one sentence.

But how were these rights to be enforced? After a bunch of other chapters—dealing with such "pressing" matters as removing from public office the kinsmen of Gerard de Athée (chapter 50), who was one of King John's favorite hit men, and releasing from hostage the sisters of King Alexander II of Scotland (chapter 59), whom John wanted to prevent from marrying French nobles with whom the rebellious Scots sought to ally—the Magna Carta creates an executive committee of twenty-five elected barons to administer its provisions. In practice, however, this proved unwieldy and ultimately unworkable.

To actually realize the promise of chapter 39, two things were, at a minimum, necessary: first, an acknowledgment by the holder of executive power that he was subordinate to the law of the land and must not only abide by it but also enforce it; and second, a mechanism by which those who were wrongly detained by the executive in violation of the law of the land might be brought before a court and freed. In the United States, part of the first requirement was met, broadly speaking, by the enactment of the Constitution and by Chief Justice John Marshall's declaration in *Marbury v. Madison* (1803) that ultimate authority for the interpretation of the Constitution lay with the Supreme Court. But this is not to say that our chief executives always accepted the rule of law. Indeed, many of our strongest executives would, on occasion, defy it. Thus, when the Supreme Court held in 1832 that Indian tribes must be treated as sovereign nations, President Andrew Jackson allegedly responded by saying: "John Marshall has made his decision; now let him enforce it." And when the Civil War broke out, President Abraham Lincoln unconstitutionally suspended the writ of habeas corpus, leading his secretary of state, William Seward, to boast to a British minister: "I can touch a bell . . . and order the imprisonment of [U.S. citizens], and no power on earth, except that of the President of the United States, can release [them]."

Which brings us to the second requirement of the rule of law, namely, a mechanism by which a court can free those who have been wrongly imprisoned by the executive in violation of the law. The chief such mechanism is the writ of habeas corpus, by which a court can require that a detained or imprisoned person be brought before a court, so that the law of the land can be applied to her case.

Contrary to what some writers and even judges have sometimes implied, the writ itself is not to be found in the Magna Carta. Indeed, it was not meaningfully developed until several centuries later. But the development of the writ was a necessary requirement if the rights put forth in chapter 39 of the Magna Carta were to be realized. As Justice John Paul Stevens, quoting Justice Robert H. Jackson, wrote for the Supreme Court in the 2004 case of *Rasul v. Bush*: "Executive imprisonment has been considered oppressive and lawless since John, at Runnymede, pledged that no free man should be imprisoned, dispossessed, outlawed, or exiled save by the judgment of his peers or by the law of the land. The judges of England developed the writ of habeas corpus largely to preserve these immunities from executive restraint."

But does the Great Writ still serve this vital function, or has it been compromised to the point of ineffectuality? I suggest that there is some cause for concern, and in that regard, I would mention two rather different examples: the detention camp at Guantánamo and the statute known as the Antiterrorism and Effective Death Penalty Act of 1996 (AEDPA).

In some respects, the legal history of the Guantánamo detention camp illustrates the continuing power of not just the writ of habeas corpus but also the Magna Carta. In the four years between 2004 and 2008, the Supreme Court considered four cases involving Guantánamo, culminating in the great decision *Boumediene v. Bush*. The plaintiff, Lakhdar Boumediene, had filed a habeas petition in federal district court, alleging that he was not in fact an enemy combatant and was being detained at Guantánamo without being given any opportunity to prove his innocence in a court of law. But in reaction to earlier petitions from Guantánamo detainees, Congress had passed a statute providing that "no court, justice, or judge shall have jurisdiction to hear or consider an application for a writ of habeas corpus filed by or on behalf of an alien detained . . . as an enemy combatant."

In a 5–4 decision, the Supreme Court held the statute unconstitutional. Writing for the majority, Justice Anthony Kennedy expressly relied on the role of the writ in enforcing the fundamental principle of chapter 39 of the Magna Carta that no one may be imprisoned except by the law of the land. While, under Article I, Section 9 of the Constitution, Congress, unlike the president, had the power to suspend the writ, Congress could do so only in "cases of rebellion or invasion," neither of which were present in the contemporary American situation. And, the Court continued, the writ extended not just to American citizens but also to aliens being held on U.S. territory, which Guantánamo was for all practical purposes.

As a theoretical matter, it is hard to overestimate the importance of *Boumediene*, for it asserted the power of the Court to guarantee the right to the writ of habeas corpus, and hence the right to the protection of the laws, even in situations arising from the so-called war on terror. One has only to contrast *Boumediene* with the failure of the Supreme Court to hold Lincoln's suspension of the writ unconstitutional until the Civil War was over, not to mention its shameful validation of the detention of Japanese Americans during World War II, to see how groundbreaking was the Court's decision in *Boumediene*. And the force of the Court's reasoning lay, first and foremost, in its reliance on the principles set forth in chapter 39 of the Magna Carta and its recognition of the essential role of habeas corpus in making those principles a reality. As Justice Kennedy wrote for the Court: "Magna Carta decreed that no man would be imprisoned contrary to the law of the land. . . . Important as the principle was, the Barons at Runnymede prescribed no specific legal process to enforce it. . . . [But] gradually the writ of habeas corpus became the means by which the promise of Magna Carta was fulfilled." It was to fulfill that promise that the Court, in *Boumediene*, rejected Congress's attempt to deny habeas relief to the prisoners in Guantánamo.

As a practical matter, however, the effect of *Boumediene* has been much more limited. In 2019, more than a decade later—despite former president Obama's pledge to shut down Guantánamo and free its detainees—forty prisoners remained in detention there. Most of them have never had access to a regular federal court (as opposed to military tribunals), and half of them have never been charged with any crime in the several decades that they have been there. And in every case in which any of these so-called forever prisoners—neither charged with a crime nor cleared for release—has filed a habeas petition, the government has opposed the petition, arguing that the resolution of such petitions should await the outcome of the pledge to close Guantánamo (which Congress, not to mention the Trump administration, has steadfastly opposed). And in virtually all such cases, the lower courts have acquiesced in this opposition or otherwise disposed of the habeas petitions without reaching the merits. The result is that opposition from the government, combined with repeated congressional opposition to the detainees' release, rather obvious foot-dragging by the Department of Defense, and a failure of the lower federal courts to intervene, has rendered the promise of *Boumediene* materially unfulfilled.

This brings me to my second example. The ability of Congress and the executive to effectively hamstring habeas relief is nowhere better illustrated than in the case of AEDPA. This statute was enacted, with strong bipartisan support, in 1996, and although the title of the act begins with the word "Antiterrorism," the rest of the title, "Effective Death Penalty Act," gives away the statute's primary immediate purpose: to reduce the ability of state prisoners facing the death penalty to obtain federal habeas relief.

Specifically, even before the Innocence Project revealed that dozens of state prisoners sentenced to death were factually innocent of the crimes of which they were accused, the federal courts were sufficiently skeptical about the processes used by many states that they granted federal habeas relief in a substantial number of such cases, leading to, if nothing else, substantial delays. An avowed purpose of AEDPA was to narrow federal habeas relief so that more such people could be promptly executed.

More broadly, the purpose of AEDPA was to reduce access to the federal courts by those convicted of any kind of crime in state courts, by limiting the scope of habeas review. To put this in perspective, the mid-1990s were the heyday of the so-called war on crime that led to mandatory minimum sentences and other onerous statutes designed to reduce rising crime rates and that resulted in the devastating mass incarceration of which many Americans are now beginning to become aware. Also, as more and more persons were incarcerated, many for prolonged terms, more and more habeas petitions were filed, leading to calls from even the judiciary to find ways to stem this flood.

Ironically, the statistics I have seen suggest that AEDPA has led not to a decrease in habeas petitions, but only to a decrease in the percentage of successful petitions. Even before the enactment of AEDPA, certain decisions of the Rehnquist Court had narrowed the reach of those Warren Court cases (including, most famously, *Miranda v. Arizona*) that had extended fundamental due process to the states, so that successful habeas petitions had declined prior to AEDPA's enactment to only 1 percent of those filed. But after AEDPA was passed, successful habeas petitions declined to a minuscule one-third of 1 percent. Why this precipitous decline?

First and foremost, it is the result of AEDPA's requirement that a habeas petition not be granted unless the state court decision that is being challenged is either contrary to or an unreasonable application of Supreme Court precedent. The Supreme Court has repeatedly interpreted this requirement so as to limit successful habeas petitions to those in which the alleged violations are so blatant as to be totally indefensible. The practical effect is to halt the prior federal practice of employing habeas review to bring new conditions of fairness to the steamroller systems of criminal justice found in too many states.

In addition to severely limiting the scope of habeas review, AEDPA greatly narrows habeas in other ways. For example, it requires total exhaustion of state review before the petition can be filed, and then requires that the petition be filed within one year of that exhaustion. As a result, 22 percent of all habeas filings are dismissed as untimely. AEDPA also places stringent restrictions on the petitioner's ability to file a second or subsequent habeas petition; it limits the circumstances under which a federal district court can convene an evidentiary hearing to assess any factual issues raised by the petition; and it places numerous other hypertechnical hurdles in the way of habeas review of the merits.

Often the only way to overcome these technical hurdles is to allege ineffective assistance of counsel. For example, if the failure to exhaust state remedies, or to raise a crucial issue while pursuing state remedies, is a function of counsel's failure to do so, then a habeas petition alleging ineffective assistance of counsel may serve to excuse these failings. The result is that an increasing number of instances of habeas review that get beyond procedural defects focus on whether defense counsel acted properly, rather than on whether the state's own practices and procedures are fair. Although such cases are often categorized by government statisticians as "reaching the merits," in fact such cases do little to change substantive law.

This does not appear particularly to bother the Supreme Court, which has, on the whole, been supportive of AEDPA against the few attacks that have made it to the top court. Perhaps this is because AEDPA serves as a protector of states' rights, a cause close to the heart of the Court's conservative majority, which views the right of individual states to exercise plenary oversight of their criminal justice systems as fundamental to federalism. It is worth noting in this connection that *Boumediene* was solely concerned with federal power.

The result is that in most criminal cases today, the real law of the land, so far as fundamental fairness is concerned, is the law of each individual state, bereft of any effective federal oversight. More fundamentally, what this means is that Congress, with the Supreme Court's acquiescence, has arrogated to itself the power to greatly limit the scope of habeas relief. This, I respectfully suggest, is totally inconsistent with the fundamental principles enunciated in chapter 39 of the Magna Carta and once thought to inhere in the Constitution of the United States. And its practical effect is to diminish the power of the courts to overturn wrongful convictions, to ensure due process, or simply to make sure that the rule of law is more than an empty phrase.

10

THE WAR ON TERROR'S WAR ON LAW

The full name of the awful AEDPA statute discussed in chapter 9 is the Antiterrorism and Effective Death Penalty Act. The title was designed for maximum political impact. Who could be against antiterrorism? And for most people the death penalty was a good thing, the effect of which had been undercut by endless delays in the courts, delays that AEDPA sought to end. But it was all for show. In this chapter, I evaluate how something as laudable as the war on terror has too often been used as an excuse for courts to avoid applying the Constitution; and in chapter 11, I discuss the Supreme Court's undue subservience to the executive branch.

It is a historical fact that when the word "war" is uttered, the rule of law often implodes, with courts frequently employing sophistry to avoid any interference with government misconduct. To take an obvious example, during World War II the Roosevelt administration interned thousands of American citizens of Japanese descent solely on the basis of their ancestry, and the Supreme Court, in an opinion by Justice Hugo Black, upheld this patently unconstitutional confinement by simply repeating the mantra that, in time of war, total deference (unchecked and unbalanced) is due the military.

During the same war, the U.S. troops fighting Nazi racism were, without judicial interference, segregated by color. Even the 1940 draft law, which stated that "in the selection and training of men under this Act, . . . there shall be no discrimination against any person on account of race or color," was held by the Second Circuit Court of Appeals not to prohibit separate draft quotas for whites and Blacks, since "the Army executives are to decide the Army's needs."

The so-called war on terror declared by President George W. Bush soon after September 11, 2001, has already lasted more than four times as long as the American involvement in World War II, with no end in sight. By its shapeless and secretive nature, it tends to generate amorphous fears and shrouded responses that compromise our freedoms in ways that we may only dimly recognize but that create troubling precedents for the future. And so far, the federal courts have done precious little to challenge these incursions.

One of the voices decrying this judicial failure is that of Owen Fiss, a very distinguished Yale law professor, to whom I must pay homage for getting me thinking more about these issues. For over the past dozen years, Fiss has written one essay after another exposing the shallowness of the judicial response to executive excesses committed in the name of national security.

A few examples will illustrate the concern. First, there is the CIA's use of torture following September 11. One may assume for the sake of argument that torture may sometimes be effective in extracting information that cannot be obtained by ordinary interrogation—although most studies suggest that its main effect is to force the victim to tell his torturer what he believes the torturer wants to hear. Indeed, historically, one of torture's most prominent uses has been to coerce false confessions, as in the show trials of the Stalinist period.

In any case, torture, regardless of whether its perceived benefits are real, has been condemned from the earliest days of the American republic. Most scholars agree that it was revulsion at the English kings' use of torture that led to enactment of the Fifth Amendment's prohibition against compelled self-incrimination and also played a part in the enactment of the Eighth Amendment's prohibition of cruel and unusual punishment. Evidence of Americans' continuing abhorrence of torture can also be found in numerous current statutes: for example, torturing a victim before murdering him is one of the "aggravating factors" that, under current federal law, warrants the death penalty.

Most directly applicable, in 1988 the United States signed and in 1994 ratified the United Nations Convention Against Torture, which thereby became a binding part of our law. Article 1 of the convention defines torture to encompass, among other things, "any act by which severe pain or suffering, whether physical or mental, is intentionally inflicted on a person for such purposes as obtaining from him or a third person information or a confession." Article 2 requires each signatory state to "take effective legislative, administrative, judicial or other measures to prevent acts of torture *in any territory under its jurisdiction*" (emphasis added). Article 2 also provides that "no exceptional circumstances whatsoever, whether a state of war or a threat of war, internal political stability or any other public emergency, may be invoked as a justification of torture."

Although the language in Article 2 italicized above might seem to permit a government agent operating abroad to make use of torture, in 1994, Congress, as part of the legislation implementing the convention, enacted section 2340A of the Federal

Criminal Code, which, among other things, prohibits any U.S. agent operating even "outside the United States" from inflicting torture on any person within his custody or physical control. Yet following September 11, CIA agents working abroad subjected suspected terrorists to waterboarding—a technique derived from the Spanish Inquisition in which water is forced into the nose and mouth of the subject so as to induce the perception of suffocating or drowning.

Waterboarding is clearly torture. Nonetheless, legal memoranda prepared by senior Justice Department officials shortly after September 11 purported to justify its use by arguing that the convention's definition of torture covered only "the worst forms of cruel, inhuman, or degrading treatment or punishment," and that "physical pain amounting to torture must be equivalent in intensity to the pain accompanying serious physical injury, such as organ failure, impairment of bodily function, or even death." As for mental suffering, to constitute torture it must, according to the memoranda, be of a kind that leads to psychological harm lasting "for months or even years."

Since, however, it is up to the judiciary to make the final determination of what a law means, one might have imagined that once the CIA's waterboarding was made public, a court would then have decided whether or not it constituted torture under section 2340A. But this did not occur, in part because the government also took the position that the CIA's waterboarding, as an instrument in the war on terror, was exempt from judicial review.

After some uncertainty, this exemption from judicial review of any decision to waterboard became the Bush administration's position at the highest levels and was effectively reiterated in 2005, in response to Congress's passage of the Detainee Treatment Act, which, among other things, provided that "no person in the custody or under the effective control of the Department of

Defense" shall be subjected to certain specified "technique[s] of interrogation," which included waterboarding. In addition to maintaining that the legislation did not apply to the CIA, President Bush, in signing the bill, asserted his power to interpret it "consistent with the constitutional limitations on judicial power"—a clear suggestion that his interpretations were exempt from judicial review. In effect, he was saying, "If we decide to waterboard, no court can say us nay."

As it happened, this supposed exemption was never put to the test as far as CIA waterboarding was concerned. Rather, the issue was resolved politically. Specifically, President Obama, soon after taking office in 2009, banned the use of waterboarding even by the CIA, and Congress effectively codified this order in 2015. Despite rumors, moreover, there have been no verified reports of CIA waterboarding since 2003. To be sure, President Trump has declared his support for waterboarding, but he does not appear to have put that support into action. So at the moment, at least, there is nothing for a court to decide when it comes to waterboarding by U.S. agents.

Regretfully, however, President Obama's ban on waterboarding did not put an end to U.S. involvement in the use of torture as part of the war on terror. Instead, within the past decade the United States has repeatedly made use of the device known as "extraordinary rendition," by which suspected terrorists detained by the United States are turned over to police authorities in other countries that regularly employ torture as an interrogation technique.

An example is the case of Maher Arar, a dual citizen of Canada and Syria, who was thought by U.S. authorities to be a supporter of al-Qaeda. In 2002, while returning to Canada from a vacation in Tunisia, Arar had to change planes at JFK in New York. He was immediately taken into custody by U.S. agents, who held him for twelve days and then, after their interrogation apparently did not lead to the desired results, shipped him to Syria, where (he alleges) they knew he would be tortured—as he was. Eventually, he brought suit against the federal agents. But the Second Circuit Court of Appeals, in a full court decision filed in late 2009, held, by a vote of 7–4, that these facts did not constitute a claim cognizable under U.S. law because the adjudication of these claims would itself interfere with national security.

Similarly, in a case involving five former detainees who alleged that the CIA arranged for them to be flown to other countries so that they could be interrogated by torture, the Ninth Circuit Court of Appeals held in 2010, by a vote of 6–5, that the detainees' lawsuit was barred by prohibitions against exposing state secrets.

Although the split votes in these cases suggest that judicial opinion is not uniform about whether extraordinary rendition is beyond judicial scrutiny, for the time being it remains a device by which U.S. officials can effectively use the torture techniques of other countries to interrogate those suspected of aiding terrorist activity. The majority view of the judiciary is not to interfere.

If the judiciary's response to extraordinary rendition is an example of its hands-off approach to dubious practices associated with the war on terror, a different kind of judicial response, which might be described as "words without deeds," is presented by another, more familiar example: namely, detention without trial of persons alleged to be enemy combatants.

Although this practice is chiefly associated in the public mind with Guantánamo, in fact it has a more general application. The basic question is whether someone charged as an "enemy combatant"—traditionally defined as "an individual who, under the laws and customs of war, may be detained for the duration of an armed conflict"—can, because of the unconventional nature of the war on terror, be indefinitely detained in U.S. custody without receiving many of the rights guaranteed by the U.S. Constitution or, if the person is considered a prisoner of war, by the Geneva Conventions. In theory, the answer may be no; but in practice, the answer appears to be yes.

Indeed, when most of the prisoners who were held at Guantánamo were first sent there, they were kept incommunicado, and their very identities were kept secret. Having neither lawyers nor ways of communicating with the outside world, these prisoners had no ability to assert even the most basic rights. Eventually, however, a number of judges (myself included) ordered the release of the identities of the persons imprisoned at Guantánamo, and this in turn led to actions being taken on their behalf, such as, for example, by their relatives.

Ultimately, the U.S. Supreme Court, in several decisions handed down between 2004 and 2008, extended to these detainees the right to petition for a writ of habeas corpus seeking their release. But although these decisions were hailed at the time as a great victory for the rule of law, in fact, as noted in chapter 9, they have proved to be something of a hollow reed. Specifically, the lower courts, most especially the D.C. Circuit Court of Appeals, have rejected, sometimes without even considering the merits, virtually all the attempts by the Guantánamo detainees to win their release, and the Supreme Court has refused to review any of these decisions.

Furthermore, despite the original aims of the Obama administration to close down Guantánamo and release most of its prisoners who could not be tried in federal court—aims that Congress has repeatedly endeavored to thwart and that the Trump administration wholly rejected—there remain at Guantánamo even now several dozen so-called forever prisoners who have never been adjudged guilty of misconduct by any court established under Article III of the Constitution, let alone a jury.

Of course, if these detainees are viewed as prisoners of war, they should, under the Geneva Conventions, be released at the conclusion of active hostilities. But given the vague, expanding way in which the war on terror has come to be viewed, the conclusion of active hostilities may never arrive. Moreover, since the detainees are not clearly identified as actors for a state, they well may not qualify as prisoners of war.

Regardless of what ultimately happens to the remaining prisoners, the failure of the Supreme Court to give practical effect to its declared right of Guantánamo detainees to bring habeas petitions sets the stage for the United States to maintain in the future a prison for hundreds, even thousands of detainees who are neither to be tried by any neutral court nor to be released, but who will just remain in prison indefinitely. There is no parallel in our history for such endless, unscrutinized detention.

These examples of government overreaching and judicial timidity regarding torture and indefinite detention have mostly involved events abroad and/or the treatment of noncitizens. But the untoward effects of prosecuting the war on terror have struck closer to home, even including some restrictions on free speech.

When I went to law school in the late 1960s, the accepted wisdom was that freedom of speech was so central to the effective functioning of our democracy that any limitation was forbidden except for speech that created a "clear and present danger," or, as the Supreme Court later put it, speech that incited "imminent lawless action." Even war or the threat or effects of war did not justify prohibiting American citizens from staunchly stating their views. Accordingly, the Alien and Sedition Acts passed by an early Congress when war with France was feared, the so-called Palmer Raids conducted against supposed anarchists in the aftermath of World War I, and the outlawing of the Communist Party during the cold war were all viewed in hindsight as violations of the First Amendment that should never be repeated.

But such examples illustrate how fragile the First Amendment can be in a time of peril. And in the 2010 Supreme Court case of *Holder v. Humanitarian Law Project*, the Court came perilously close to upholding the power of the government to criminalize any speech that could be construed as supporting a terrorist organization. The relevant statute, Section 2339B of the Federal Criminal Code, makes it a federal crime to knowingly provide material support to any entity designated by the secretary of state as a "foreign terrorist organization." The term "material support" is defined to include, among other things, providing a "service" to the organization, and thus might be read to include speaking in favor of the organization or praising any of its activities, even activities that are benign.

Because of this danger, U.S. supporters of two groups that had been designated by the secretary of state as terrorist organizations—a pro-Kurdish group in Turkey and a pro-Tamil group in Sri Lanka—sought a "declaratory judgment" (a kind of advance ruling) that they could not be prosecuted under the statute for speaking out on behalf of certain nonviolent activities of these organizations.

The Supreme Court might have granted the plaintiffs' application by simply construing the statute not to include speech. Instead, in a 6–3 decision written by Chief Justice Roberts, the Supreme Court in *Holder v. Humanitarian Law Project* took the position that, while the statute could not criminalize speech independently initiated by the U.S. supporters of these organizations, it could reach advocacy "performed in coordination with, or at the direction of" the terrorist organization, since such speech would constitute a "service" to the organization. It would not matter, moreover, that the speech only advocated the peaceful activities of the organizations in question, since even such advocacy would help the organization in its overall activities, including acts of terrorism.

From the modest perspective of a lowly district judge, it seems to me that the distinction between "independent" free speech on behalf of an organization and speech "coordinated" with the organization is highly questionable. Would the tens of thousands of Irish American citizens who in the 1980s supported the Irish independence goals of Sinn Féin, but not its more extreme tactics, have been liable for criminal prosecution under this statute if they had expressed their favorable views of its goals in response to a Sinn Féin request to "show your support"?

Or, to give another kind of example, would someone who believed that a given organization had been wrongly designated by the secretary of state as a terrorist organization be subject to criminal prosecution if, with the organization's approval, he placed an ad in *The New York Times* setting out the reasons why the secretary got it wrong?

What plainly underlies the Court's opinion is the implicit premise that the war on terror justifies this serious chilling of free speech. Thus, for example, the chief justice writes that "the Government's interest in combating terrorism is an urgent objective of the highest order." Quite aside from the fact that, under the standard of "clear and present danger," it is difficult to see the urgency of any U.S. interest in combating Kurdish and Tamil insurgency, the statement is, in context, a thinly disguised suggestion that advocacy on behalf of any disfavored organization labeled by the secretary as terrorist is subject to censorship. Such a view would have fully justified the British pre-Revolutionary censorship that gave rise to the First Amendment.

Fortunately, the blank check of censorship authorized by the aforementioned Supreme Court decision has for the most part not yet been cashed by the Department of Justice. Under the Obama administration, there were only a couple of prosecutions under Section 2339B for speech activities, and those involved direct incitements to violence. But who knows what current and future administrations might do?

The overall point is that, in the absence of more effective judicial scrutiny, the government will always use the excuse of war to take authoritarian measures that no other excuse could hope to justify. Such measures might well be open to serious question even against the background of a conventional war. But the unique features of the war on terror—its uncertain legal status, its shifting, nonstate adversaries, its untraditional methods, its unclear goals, and its highly indefinite duration—all combine to make it difficult for the courts to intervene. Yet the judiciary would seem to be the branch of government best situated to place meaningful limits on the wide-ranging and sometimes horrifying government activities supposedly justified by this strange war. We judges avoid that duty to our, and our country's, peril.

11

THE SUPREME COURT'S UNDUE SUBSERVIENCE TO THE EXECUTIVE BRANCH

In the current political climate, federal courts are often viewed as the only branch of government likely to impose checks on executive overreach. This may be true at the lower level of the federal courts; but, as previous chapters suggest, the current Supreme Court has often taken a narrow view of its role in this regard, choosing to be largely subservient to the executive when it comes to everything from torture to the death penalty. I would go further and suggest that this is something of an old story, one that traces back to the earliest days of the Court—even to the days of Chief Justice John Marshall, who is generally regarded as the progenitor of federal judicial power.

George Washington was an inspiring leader, and Thomas Jefferson could turn a phrase; but to federal judges, the greatest of the Founding Fathers was undoubtedly John Marshall, chief justice of the United States from 1801 to 1835, who forged the role of federal law in American life.

In his four-volume *Life of John Marshall* (1916), Albert J.

Beveridge writes, "The work of John Marshall has been of supreme importance in the development of the American Nation, and its influence grows as time passes." But Beveridge then cautions that "such exalted, if vague, encomium has been paid him, that, even to the legal profession, he has become a kind of mythical being, endowed with virtues and wisdom not of this earth." Nonetheless, Beveridge's biography is largely a panegyric to Marshall, and the titles of more recent biographies, such as Jean Edward Smith's *John Marshall: Definer of a Nation* (1996) and Harlow Giles Unger's *John Marshall: The Chief Justice Who Saved the Nation* (2014), indicate how much Marshall is still viewed with an awe that may inhibit critical thinking.

Here, I take the liberty of suggesting that Marshall, while hugely instrumental in assuring for the federal judiciary its limited supervisory role over the legislative branch, exhibited a subservience to the executive branch that continues to haunt us.

But, first, a brief background on Marshall the man. Certainly there was a heroic aspect to Marshall's rise to prominence. Although it is commonplace to think of him as a member of the colonial Virginia aristocracy, in fact he was the proverbial poor cousin. This was because his maternal grandmother, though born a Randolph (a fabled First Family of Virginia), was disinherited after being caught in flagrante delicto with a Scottish minister, James Keith.

Banished to the barely developed wilds of western Virginia, the two eventually married, but the taint of scandal continued to hang over their children, including Marshall's mother, Mary Keith, who, bereft of money and connections, wound up marrying a farmer of modest means. In frontier fashion, they lived in a two-room log cabin in Germantown, Virginia, while raising fifteen children, of whom John Marshall, born in 1755, was the eldest.

Unlike his second cousin Thomas Jefferson, who was born

on a large plantation and received years of private tutoring before entering the College of William and Mary at age sixteen, Marshall was largely self-taught and had no more than one year of formal schooling. His first job of any consequence was as a soldier in the Revolutionary War, in which, during the winter at Valley Forge, he met George Washington, who thereafter served as one of his mentors. (Years later, Marshall wrote a five-volume biography of Washington that, as another of Marshall's recent biographers, Professor Joel Richard Paul of Hastings Law School, puts it, "was the first of many presidential biographies to flop.")

Following the Revolutionary War, Marshall enrolled in the law curriculum at the College of William and Mary, but again unlike Jefferson (who graduated from the college with highest honors), he lasted only six weeks before dropping out. Nevertheless, he passed the bar examination and became licensed to practice law in Virginia.

On these limited foundations, Marshall built a command of the law and a skill in oral and written advocacy that quickly made him a leader of the Virginia bar. In the manner of the day, his law practice was extremely varied, involving everything from drawing up simple wills, deeds, and contracts to negotiating and, where necessary, litigating complex commercial matters, with the occasional criminal case thrown in for good measure. Even in a bar that also featured Jefferson, Edmund Randolph, Patrick Henry, and James Monroe, Marshall quickly established a reputation as one of the best. Whether this bespeaks genius or simply perseverance, there can be no doubt that he was an early example of that idealized American prototype, the self-made man. It also did not hurt that, by all accounts, he was convivial, honest, dependable, good-looking, self-effacing, well connected, and capable of inspiring confidence.

Like many other lawyers, Marshall had a penchant for politics, and in the turmoil that eventually led to the drafting of the Constitution in 1787 and the subsequent battle over its ratification, he sided with the Federalists in favoring a stronger central government, while many prominent Virginians—cognizant of Virginia's status as the largest and wealthiest of the former thirteen colonies—backed the anti-Federalists in wanting the states to retain near-total sovereignty. When the Federalists prevailed and the Constitution was ratified, Marshall became, in effect, the Virginian to whom the Federalists (whose primary base was in New England) would turn when they needed a local man to articulate their cause.

Eventually, however, Marshall rose to national prominence, largely as a result of the so-called XYZ Affair. In 1797, newly elected president John Adams sent Marshall and two other envoys, Charles Pinckney and Elbridge Gerry, to Paris to try to negotiate an end to French depredations of U.S. shipping that were a side effect of the ongoing war between Britain and France. But when the Americans reached Paris, they were approached in turn by three emissaries—X, Y, and Z—of the French foreign minister, Charles Maurice de Talleyrand-Périgord, who demanded a personal bribe as the price of an audience. When it subsequently became known that the Americans had stoutly refused to pay any bribe, even at the cost of their mission, they became national heroes.

After Marshall returned from France in June 1798, parades were held in his honor and crowds lined the streets. Less than a year later, Marshall was elected to Congress from a Virginia district that was otherwise staunchly Republican (the Republicans, or Jeffersonians, being the successors to the anti-Federalists). And just a year after that, in May 1800, Adams appointed Marshall secretary of state.

Not long after Marshall took office, however, the Republicans swamped the Federalists in the national elections of November 1800, winning majorities in both houses of Congress. In the subsequent voting in the electoral college, Jefferson, after initially being tied with Aaron Burr, was elected president. (A few years later, Marshall, as chief justice, would preside over the trial of Burr for treason, which ended when Marshall, to the dismay of Jefferson, directed the jury to acquit Burr.)

In response to these Republican victories, the lame-duck Federalists decided to pack the federal courts with as many of their own as they could induce to take on judicial appointments. First in line was Marshall, who on January 27, 1801, was confirmed by the departing Federalist Senate as the fourth chief justice of the United States.

Marshall, like many other notable lawyers, had previously refused nomination to the Supreme Court. Indeed, it was no great thing to be a Supreme Court justice in those days, for the Court's docket was largely limited to maritime cases; the real action was in the state courts. The justices also had to live together in boardinghouses and ride circuit over muddy roads and difficult terrain to hear cases in various locations far from Washington.

In his biography (entitled *Without Precedent*), Paul speculates that Marshall accepted the appointment as chief justice "out of a sense of duty." Specifically, Paul argues, Marshall viewed Jefferson as a hypocrite and a demagogue:

> For Marshall's whole life, from the poverty of his boyhood to his service in the Continental Army to his political fights in Virginia, he had been locked in a bitter rivalry with the cousin who was born with all the advantages that Marshall's family had been denied. . . . [In Marshall's view,] Jefferson was a radical ideologue, and Marshall had witnessed how French ideologues

had undermined the rule of law. Jefferson lacked genuine empathy and embodied precisely the kind of elitism that he attacked in theory. In these circumstances, Marshall, in accepting appointment as chief justice, "saw himself as defending the Constitution against the onslaught of the Jeffersonians."

Perhaps. But as Paul also mentions, Marshall's political career was likely finished, as his district in Virginia had returned to being solidly Republican.

Moreover, the Supreme Court position would provide financial security, since Marshall's law practice, largely held in abeyance during his sojourn in Washington, was unlikely to earn him as much as the chief justice's salary of $4,000. Perhaps, too, he was not as embarrassed as he professed to be about becoming a national celebrity, and was not immune to the type of political ambition now known as "Potomac fever."

Marshall had plenty of company among Federalists who accepted these lame-duck appointments. The outgoing Federalist Congress created sixteen federal circuit judgeships and forty-two new positions for federal justices of the peace (low-level judicial functionaries). All these positions were filled by Federalists nominated and confirmed in Adams's last days in office, giving rise to the satiric title of "midnight judges." In Jefferson's view, "The Federalists have retired into the judiciary as a stronghold, and from that battery all the works of republicanism are to be beaten down and erased."

Both Jefferson and Marshall thus viewed Marshall's ascent to the Supreme Court as part of a battle for the soul of America, however much it might also appear as part of a family feud. But whatever his motivations, Marshall's timing in accepting the position was impeccable, for during his tenure the size and scope of the Court's work expanded greatly, with a concomitant rise in its power and importance. For example, as the nation's economy began to grow and become more interconnected, great questions arose about whether control over interstate commerce was to be relegated to the states, to the federal government, or to some combination of the two—questions the Marshall Court definitively answered in favor of federal control in cases such as *Gibbons v. Ogden* (1824). Similarly, as the federal treasury, under Alexander Hamilton's leadership, played an ever-larger part in banking, questions arose as to whether the federal power to tax and to issue currency indirectly conferred a power to create a federal bank, a question the Court again definitively answered in favor of a broad application of federal power in *McCulloch v. Maryland* (1819). In these and many other ways, the Marshall Court greatly enhanced the power of the federal government over the states, but in the process it also enhanced the power of the federal executive.

Over the thirty-four years that Marshall was chief justice, the Supreme Court issued no fewer than 1,129 decisions. Remarkably, all but 87 of them (and all but 36 of the 547 opinions authored by Marshall) were unanimous, even though the Court was deeply divided throughout most of these years between Federalists and Republicans (who later evolved into Whigs and Democrats, respectively). This unanimity was a tribute not only to Marshall's force of personality and character but also to his zeal for achieving consensus. And as a practical matter, the seven justices having to bunk together in the same boardinghouse must have put a premium on getting along with one another. But perhaps achieving unanimity was made easier by the fact that in so many of these early cases, they were writing on a relatively blank slate, largely unhampered by binding precedents (though they would look to English law for guidance). Conscious that they were literally creating the precedents that would bind future generations, the justices as a group may have been predisposed toward compromise and consensus.

This tendency was further enhanced by an important change Marshall introduced early in his tenure. Prior to his arrival, each justice rendered a separate oral opinion in each case, this being the style in English courts. But Marshall decided that the Court's authority would be increased if it acted as a whole and issued a single opinion (or, if divided, a single majority opinion), delivered orally but then put in writing.

Too much compromise can, however, create its own problems. As a general matter, the Anglo-American legal system values consistency and predictability, while judicial decisions that lean toward compromise are often ambiguous and uncertain in their future application. The compromises forged by Marshall on the Supreme Court, although worded in the language of strong judicial oversight, sometimes entailed a barely concealed deference to unlawful executive action. Consider two of the most famous cases from Marshall's tenure: *Marbury v. Madison* (1803) and *Cherokee Nation v. Georgia* (1831).

Marbury v. Madison is typically cited as the first case in which the Supreme Court, after flatly asserting its power to be the final arbiter of the meaning of the Constitution, implemented that power of judicial review by declaring an act of Congress unconstitutional. (The Court would not do so again for another fifty-four years, in the *Dred Scott* decision.) But perhaps *Marbury v. Madison* deserves a closer look, specifically for how it deferred to the power of the president.

The facts of the case were peculiar, and today would almost certainly have led Marshall to recuse himself. The appointments of the sixteen circuit judges (including Marshall's brother James) and forty-two justices of the peace confirmed by the Federalists in the very last days of the Adams administration would not take effect until their formal commissions were signed by the president and the secretary of state (who also had to affix the Great Seal of the United States) and then delivered to the appointees. On Adams's last day in office, March 3, 1801, the outgoing secretary of state—Marshall—duly cosigned all the commissions (they had already been signed by the president) and delivered them to the sixteen circuit judges (including James Marshall), but somehow neglected to arrange for the delivery of the commissions of the forty-two justices of the peace, which were found the next day on his vacated desk at the State Department. In due course the new president, Jefferson, still furious at the Federalist takeover of the judiciary, directed Levi Lincoln, Sr., an interim secretary of state, not to deliver seventeen of these commissions, including that of William Marbury, who, joined by several of the other putative justices of the peace, then brought suit.

Marbury and his co-plaintiffs filed with the Supreme Court an emergency application familiar to lawyers to this day: an "order to show cause" demanding that James Madison (who had now taken up the post of secretary of state) give reasons why he should not be mandamused, that is, forced to deliver the commissions. In response, Madison, declining to acknowledge the Court's jurisdiction, chose not to appear, though he did send a lawyer. President Jefferson let it be known in advance that if the Court ordered him or Madison to deliver the commissions, the response would be a refusal.

The Court nonetheless held a four-day evidentiary hearing, during which it had to be proved that the plaintiffs had been confirmed as justices of the peace and that their commissions had been properly signed and sealed. But the actual signatory, John Marshall, could not be called as a witness, since he was presiding over the case as chief justice. Therefore, plaintiffs' counsel introduced an affidavit from James Marshall, averring on personal knowledge that the commissions had been signed and sealed. The affidavit was most likely a fabrication, as James Marshall probably had no personal knowledge of whether his brother had signed the commissions for the justices of the peace. Nevertheless, John Marshall, sitting as the presiding judge, accepted his brother's affidavit in evidence.

A few days after the hearing, Marshall delivered the opinion of a unanimous Supreme Court. On the one hand, the Court held that the plaintiffs had a right to their commissions and that Madison's refusal to deliver them or recognize the plaintiffs as justices of the peace was flatly unlawful: "To withhold the commission, therefore, is an act deemed by the Court not warranted by law, but violative of a vested legal right." Furthermore, Marshall stated, "the Government of the United States has been emphatically termed a government of laws, and not of men. It will certainly cease to deserve this high appellation, if the laws furnish no remedy for the violation of a vested legal right."

According to the Court, the appropriate way to remedy the violation was to order the executive to deliver the commissions (i.e., grant mandamus). And the Judiciary Act of 1789 (the very first judiciary act passed by Congress) expressly gave the Supreme Court that power. But under the Constitution, the jurisdiction of the Supreme Court was limited, with exceptions not here relevant, to hearing cases on appeal; and while it could therefore issue mandamus to enforce its appellate decisions, to the extent that the Judiciary Act purported to give the Court the power to grant mandamus in a non-appellate proceeding, the act was unconstitutional. Too bad for Marbury.

As Paul and others point out, if the Court lacked the power to issue mandamus in this matter, why did it not simply dismiss the petition at the outset? Why undertake a four-day hearing (with all its doubtful shenanigans) and why, in any event, declare the failure to grant the commissions unlawful, when the Court should not be even hearing the case?

The conventional answer is that Marshall glossed over all this because he wanted a vehicle for asserting the power of the Court. In Marshall's memorable words, it "is emphatically the province and duty of the judicial department to say what the law is," even if it means declaring an act of Congress unconstitutional. But this bold assertion should not wholly blind us to the fact that Marshall is here trying to have it both ways. He first declares that the executive has acted unlawfully and that the Supreme Court has the final word. But he winds up holding that the Court has no power in this case to do anything about the clear violation of law it has determined the executive to have committed.

While it has become accepted wisdom that *Marbury v. Madison* was therefore a clever ploy that asserted the Court's power while avoiding a direct confrontation with the government, I think this is only partly true. By holding an act of Congress unconstitutional, the Court definitely asserted its power to serve as a check on legislative excess, even if, somewhat ironically, the excess consisted in giving too much power to the judiciary. But how can it be said that the Court held the executive accountable to the Constitution when the opinion, having flatly determined that Madison had acted unlawfully when he refused to deliver the commissions, declined to enforce the law or vindicate the plaintiffs' acknowledged rights? Marshall had already stated in the very same opinion that if the law is to mean anything, there must be a remedy for a violation of rights; and yet the opinion nowhere indicates what remedy Marbury might avail himself of. Looked at in this way, *Marbury* can be viewed as judicial posturing that barely conceals a submission to executive power.

In fairness, it must be noted that Marshall was writing at a time when the power of the Court to actually enforce its decisions was in doubt, and this remained true throughout his tenure. In the face of issues like slavery that were increasingly tearing the nation apart, it took courage for him to continually reassert the responsibility of the Court to act as the final arbiter of the law of the land. He did so in a long series of monumental decisions, written in his inspiring and majestic prose, that in the end left no doubt that that was the Court's view.

Among much else, the Marshall Court also ratified the supremacy of the federal government over state governments in those situations where their powers overlapped, defended the property rights of individuals against intrusions by both state and federal authorities (this approach very much reflecting Marshall's Federalist views), made international law part of the law of the United States, and took an evolutionary view of the Constitution that would not be seriously questioned until the time of Justice Antonin Scalia. But few of these marvelous decisions dealt with challenges to the exercise of power by the federal executive branch.

One area where the exercise of executive power frequently did seem to run afoul of the law was in dealings with Native American tribes. Late in Marshall's tenure, this conflict came to a head in the case of *Cherokee Nation v. Georgia*. The Cherokee occupied a good deal of land in the western part of Georgia, but when gold was discovered there in 1828, Georgia seized control of their gold mines and reasserted jurisdiction over their territory. President Andrew Jackson, the former Indian fighter, announced a federal plan to forcibly remove the Cherokee to lands farther west and pushed through Congress the Indian Removal Act of 1830, which authorized him to implement his plan.

The Cherokee Nation fought back and filed a demand for injunctive relief in the Supreme Court, noting that a provision of Article III of the Constitution provides original (i.e., direct, rather than appellate) federal jurisdiction over disputes between a U.S. state and "foreign States, Citizens, or Subjects," which, the Cherokee argued, included them. Like Madison in the *Marbury* case, Georgia chose not even to appear, arguing that the Court lacked jurisdiction; and Jackson, like Jefferson before him, let it be known that he would not enforce the Court's decision if it favored the Indians.

Marshall's opinion for the Court begins in stirring fashion:

> This bill is brought by the Cherokee Nation, praying an injunction to restrain the state of Georgia from the execution of certain laws of that state, which, as is alleged, go directly to annihilate the Cherokees as a political society, and to seize, for the use of Georgia, the lands of the nation which have been assured to them by the United States in solemn treaties repeatedly made and still in force. If courts were permitted to indulge their sympathies, a case better calculated to excite them can scarcely be imagined.

But once again, as in *Marbury*, there is a catch. Even though the treaties to which Marshall makes reference clearly treat the Cherokee as an independent nation, the Cherokee are still not "a foreign state in the sense in which that term is used in the Constitution." Rather, they and other Indian tribes are "domestic dependent nations." In words that even admirers of Marshall should cringe to repeat, he writes that the tribes exist in a "state of pupilage." He then explains: "Their relation to the United States resembles that of a ward to his guardian. They look to our government for protection; rely upon its kindness and power; appeal to it for relief to their wants; and address the President as their great father."

So forget about relief from a federal court. Once again, most commentators view this as shrewd strategy, one calculated to avoid a direct confrontation with a president as popular as Jackson. But another way to look at it is that, once again, Marshall, for all his talk of judicial power, sacrificed the rights of innocent victims to Jackson's raw exercise of executive power, hypocritically suggesting that the Indians, as wards of the federal government, should look to the executive, and not the federal courts, for relief from intrusions by the states, when he had all but acknowledged that this relief was a vain hope. In light of this decision, it is hardly surprising that a few years later the federal government exercised its "kindness and power" by forcing the Cherokee to march west over the Trail of Tears, thousands of them dying along the way.

To be sure, with the benefit of hindsight, even the greatest heroes have some clay in their feet, and it is hard to think of another Supreme Court justice—not Oliver Wendell Holmes, not Louis Brandeis, not William Brennan—who so completely laid the foundations for a federal system of justice worthy of respect as Marshall did. Marshall not only empowered the federal judiciary but guided it to safety during some of the most perilous years in our nation's history. Nor do I mean to suggest that every time a federal court dares to rein in the president, it necessarily serves the public interest or is uninfluenced by the judge's political ideology. But I do suggest that, for whatever reason, the Supreme Court has frequently been far more deferential to the president than to Congress—and that this imbalance took root in the early days of the Court.

12

DON'T COUNT ON THE COURTS

As suggested in the preceding chapter, the Supreme Court, from its earliest days, has been more deferential to the executive branch of federal government than to the legislative branch. Even before John Marshall, this tendency had begun to surface. Thus, while the Constitution itself does not distinguish between the Court's powers vis-à-vis the executive and vis-à-vis the legislature, a close reading of the Federalist Papers suggests that some of the Founders—especially Alexander Hamilton—regarded the courts as more of a check on the legislative branch than on the executive branch. In Federalist No. 78, the primary Federalist Paper describing the responsibility of the judiciary, Hamilton, after characterizing the judiciary as the "least dangerous" branch (because judges have no direct power over "the sword or the purse"), writes that "the courts were designed to be an intermediate body between the people and the legislature, in order, among other things, to keep the latter within the limits assigned to their authority."

But nowhere does he mention judges' parallel responsibility to confine the executive.

According to Federalist No. 78, the courts' responsibility to hold Congress accountable is to be fulfilled through the power of judicial review of the constitutionality of legislation. But, as described in chapter 11, when this power was first and most famously exercised, in the case of *Marbury v. Madison* (1803), the Supreme Court held an act of Congress unconstitutional precisely so that the executive could proceed as it wished.

Marbury was a portent, for over the next two hundred years the Court found one way or another to avoid interfering with a wide variety of executive actions that might well be viewed as unlawful. The most defensible of these exclusions from judicial interference with executive action relates to the president's exercise of his war powers. The last thing a president and his commanders need is second-guessing by civilian courts as to the conduct of a war. But, as described in chapter 9, presidents from Abraham Lincoln to Franklin Roosevelt to George W. Bush (and beyond) have taken advantage of this deference to commit blatantly unconstitutional acts.

As mentioned in chapter 9, such acts taken in the name of the president's war powers include Lincoln's wartime suspension of the writ of habeas corpus, which the Supreme Court did not nullify until long after the Civil War; Roosevelt's internment during World War II of more than one hundred thousand Japanese Americans (most of whom were U.S. citizens), which the Court approved at the time and did not expressly question until 2018; and Bush's approval in the war on terror of torture, secret surveillance, and indefinite internment of foreigners, most of which has proved immune from challenge in the courts.

But even where no warfare of any kind is involved, virtually any lawsuit that touches on the conduct of the military is considered to be beyond the reach of the Supreme Court. A good example is *United States v. Stanley* (1987). In 1958, James B. Stanley, a serviceman, volunteered for what was ostensibly a chemical warfare testing program. In the course of the program, he was secretly given LSD as part of an army plan to test the effects of the drug on human beings. This caused him to suffer severe personality changes that led, among other things, to the dissolution of his marriage. But when he sued the government, the Supreme Court rejected his suit out of hand, holding that no lawsuit may be brought in a nonmilitary court for injuries that "arise out of or are in the course of activity incident to [military] service."

Not only have the courts determined that anything that touches on war or the military is largely beyond any meaningful judicial review, but they have also accorded similarly supine deference to any executive action that can be claimed to serve the interests of national security. In June 2017, for example, the Supreme Court heard a lawsuit, *Ziglar v. Abbasi*, brought on behalf of more than seven hundred illegal aliens rounded up after September 11 and detained, often for months, even though the government had no substantive basis for suspecting that they were in any way linked to terrorism. While being detained, they were, in the Court's own words, subjected to very "harsh conditions." For example, prison guards allegedly "slammed detainees into walls; twisted their arms, wrists, and fingers; broke their bones; referred to them as terrorists; threatened them with violence; subjected them to humiliating sexual comments; and insulted their religion." Nevertheless, the Supreme Court, overruling the Second Circuit Court of Appeals, threw out the lawsuit because, among other things, allowing such a suit "would require courts to interfere in an intrusive way with sensitive functions of the Executive Branch." Instead, the Court said, the judiciary should exercise very substantial "deference to what the Executive Branch has determined . . . is essential to national security."

Indeed, not just at the Supreme Court but in the lower federal courts as well, a talismanic invocation of national security continues to be a cloak for all kinds of executive actions that might not otherwise survive judicial review. For example, in *Merida Delgado v. Gonzales* (2005), a resident of Panama had his flight training in Oklahoma cut short after the attorney general determined that he was a "risk to aviation or national security." There was no apparent basis for that determination beyond the fact that Delgado was a noncitizen and that one of the participants in the September 11 attack had been trained in the same school. But the Tenth Circuit Court of Appeals threw out Delgado's suit, stating that "it is rarely appropriate for courts to intervene in matters closely related to national security."

Even when neither war nor national security is involved, almost as much deference to executive action has been given in cases that touch on the power of the president to conduct foreign affairs. For example, in *City of New York v. Permanent Mission of India to the United Nations et al.* (2008), New York City sought to recover property taxes owed by various foreign governments on the many floors of New York buildings owned by those governments that were not being used for diplomatic offices. The case was originally before me, and I ruled largely in favor of the city. But while the case was pending on appeal, the U.S. State Department issued a notice entirely exempting from property taxes any real estate owned by any foreign government if any portion was used for diplomatic purposes or even just for housing staff. That was good enough for the Second Circuit Court of Appeals to reverse the decision, stating that deference to the State

Department must be "especially substantial . . . [in] an area bound up with [unspecified] security concerns and issues of reciprocity among nations."

In most of the examples given above, the courts, while nominally permitting challenges to executive action to be heard, have largely ignored the substantive merits and instead accorded near-total deference to the executive. But the courts have also created a series of doctrines that deny review altogether. The two most prominent such doctrines—the requirement of "standing" and the exclusion of judicial review of "political questions"—are as murky in their definitions as they are frequently unfortunate in their consequences.

Under the doctrine of standing, no one can challenge executive action in federal court who has not, as a direct result of the action, personally and uniquely suffered a concrete past or present injury. For example, in *Warth v. Seldin* (1975), low- and moderate-income residents of Rochester, New York, who were effectively barred from moving to the nearby suburb of Penfield because of its restrictive zoning ordinances and their exclusionary application, sought to challenge this practice in federal court. But the Supreme Court held that they lacked standing to sue, because "the asserted harm is a 'generalized grievance' shared in substantially equal measure by all or a large class of citizens." In other words, if unlawful executive regulations or conduct broadly affect enough people, then none can sue.

The result is that huge swaths of executive misconduct cannot be challenged in federal court. And one might add that even when a victim of government misconduct can somehow find a way to satisfy the narrow standing doctrine, he or she will very likely be unable to obtain any monetary relief from the perpetrator of the misconduct, due to other judicially created doctrines that accord total immunity to prosecutors, administrators, various other government executives, and the government as a whole, as well as partial but substantial immunity to the police.

These latter doctrines, though they are often rationalized in terms of freeing executive action from stifling burdens, ultimately derive from archaic notions of sovereign immunity that can be traced back to the concept of an absolute monarchy in which "the king can do no wrong." But in practice these immunities mean that even those rare lawsuits against government misconduct that somehow manage to make it past the barrier of standing often result in hollow victories that have limited deterrent effect.

Equally broad, and equally nebulous, is the doctrine that excludes from judicial review so-called political questions. No one really knows what this doctrine means. The closest the Supreme Court has ever come to defining it was in a rambling, convoluted sentence in *Baker v. Carr* (1962):

> Prominent on the surface of any case held to involve a political question is found a textually demonstrable commitment of the issue to a coordinate political department; or a lack of judicially discoverable and manageable standards for resolving it; or the impossibility of deciding without an initial policy determination of a kind clearly for nonjudicial discretion; or the impossibility of a court's undertaking independent resolution without expressing lack of the respect due coordinate branches of government; or an unusual need for unquestioning adherence to a political decision already made; or the potentiality of embarrassment from multifarious pronouncements by various departments on one question.

If you don't understand that, you're not alone. For example, the Supreme Court has sometimes held that challenges to gerrymandering are political questions that cannot be adjudicated by a federal court, and other times the opposite. In practice, the "political question" doctrine is so unclear that you can never tell when a federal court will invoke it or not; but it provides a handy excuse for a court to duck a difficult issue when it chooses to.

The foregoing examples by no means exhaust the numerous ways the courts have chosen to remove themselves from meaningful review of executive excess, even when it violates the Constitution. For example, under the Supreme Court's decision in *Chevron USA., Inc. v. Natural Resources Defense Council, Inc.* (1984), the federal courts accord very substantial deference to an administrative agency's interpretation of applicable laws and rules. This seems miles removed from Chief Justice John Marshall's famous statement in *Marbury v. Madison*, quoted in chapter 11, that it "is emphatically the province and duty of the judicial department to say what the law is."

Not all of these limitations on judicial review of executive action have been initiated by judges. Congress has not been shy about limiting the jurisdiction of federal courts to review unconstitutional actions by state officials. Under the Antiterrorism and Effective Death Penalty Act of 1996 (AEDPA), discussed in previous chapters, federal review of wrongful state confinement is available only if the state court's approval of the alleged misconduct is contrary to already "clearly established" federal law. If AEDPA had been in effect forty years earlier, it would have prevented the Warren Court from ever reaching many of its most groundbreaking decisions, such as *Gideon v. Wainwright* (1963), which required states to provide legal counsel to defendants who could not pay for lawyers themselves.

But most of the restrictions described above have been created by the Supreme Court. As Justice Louis Brandeis noted as early as 1936, "The Court [has] developed, for its own governance in the cases confessedly within its jurisdiction, a series of rules under which it has avoided passing upon a large part of all the constitutional questions pressed upon it for decision." As shown above, this avoidance is particularly acute when it comes to reviewing executive actions. One must therefore ask: Why have judges chosen to put such severe limits on their power to decide whether executive actions comply with the law?

One obvious reason is that the courts are ultimately dependent on the executive to enforce judicial decisions. As Hamilton put it in Federalist No. 78, "The judiciary . . . may truly be said to have neither force nor will, but merely judgment; and must ultimately depend upon the aid of the executive arm even for the efficacy of its judgments." As discussed in chapter 11, before *Marbury v. Madison* was decided, President Jefferson had let it be known that if the Court ordered Madison to deliver Marbury's commission, he would refuse to enforce the decision. And, as noted in chapter 9, Andrew Jackson, when hearing that the Supreme Court had rendered one of its few decisions favoring Native Americans, is said to have remarked: "John Marshall has made his decision; now let him enforce it."

More recently, it has been suggested that President Eisenhower at first temporized before finally deciding to send troops to Little Rock, Arkansas, to enforce school integration. Governors of many southern states had already announced that they would refuse to enforce it, so that, if Eisenhower had not finally acted, the most important Supreme Court decision of the last century, *Brown v. Board of Education* (1954), would have been rendered a nullity. In the back of their minds, I suggest, most federal judges recognize the need to remain on good terms with the executive if their judgments are to be enforced.

Enforcement aside, the Supreme Court has frequently expressed its desire to remain above the fray, so as not to be perceived as a politically driven body but rather as one objectively finding and applying the law. This quaint notion, regularly contradicted in cases ranging from *Bush v. Gore* (2000) to *Citizens United v. Federal Election Commission* (2010), may still have some force in less controversial cases. And it certainly is true that the constitutional doctrine of separation of powers counsels against the Court becoming any kind of quasi-legislative body.

This has led some judges (notably Justice Felix Frankfurter) and legal scholars (notably the late Yale law professor Alexander Bickel) to praise the "passive virtue" of courts avoiding the rendering of legal decisions in controversial issues on which no national consensus has yet emerged. In Bickel's words, the question for courts in choosing whether to decide an issue should be "not only which principles and how, but also, when and in what circumstances." Frankfurter went even further, and, in one of the Court's decisions refusing to address gerrymandering, simply concluded that "courts ought not to enter this political thicket."

According to this approach, in other words, a federal court should not decide a dispute that the Constitution gives it the power to decide. This seems, on its face, a dereliction of duty: indeed, the Supreme Court, in numerous other cases, has frequently referred to its "unflagging duty" to exercise its jurisdiction. (Consistency is not the Court's strong point.) In any case, such conscious avoidance frequently fails to achieve its intended purpose, for it can be interpreted by the public as the equivalent of making a decision. Chief Justice Roger Taney is said to have believed that his 1857 *Dred Scott* decision—which, by denying Scott standing to sue on the ground that the Constitution did not extend the rights of citizenship to slaves, ducked the main issue of whether a slave who went to free territory thereby became a free man—avoided embroiling the Court in the slavery controversy. But in fact the effect was just the opposite, as the decision was rightly seen as an endorsement of slavery and was roundly denounced throughout the North.

Most of all, the "above the fray" approach is hardly consistent with the fundamental notion that the judiciary should serve as a check on other branches of government and make sure they are adhering to the law. This is not an easy or popular task, but often there is no one but the courts to assume it. And as Harry Truman famously said, "If you can't stand the heat, get out of the kitchen."

Nevertheless, now that the courts have created, largely on their own initiative, so many doctrines that limit their review of executive action, it would not be easy to change overnight. This is especially true under the Anglo-American common law mode of jurisprudence, in which great weight is given to prior precedents, so as to afford certainty and predictability in a judicial system that is much less bound by written legal codes than the so-called civil law systems of Europe and much of Asia.

Still, doctrines that are made by judges can be unmade by judges. And there have been times when executive excess has been extreme enough to convince the Supreme Court to intervene. This was true, for example, when in 1952 President Truman tried to use his "war powers" to justify his seizure of the U.S. steel mills during a prolonged strike. Although Truman claimed the seizure was necessary to ensure adequate supplies of steel to the military, which was then engaged in the Korean War, the Supreme Court demurred: "Even though 'theatre of war' be an expanding concept, we cannot with faithfulness to our constitutional system hold that the Commander in Chief of the Armed Forces has the ultimate power as such to take possession of private property in order to keep labor disputes from stopping production." Similarly, when President Nixon, during the Watergate investigation, refused to turn over the tapes he had made of his daily conversations, claiming that to do so would violate both executive privilege and the separation of powers, the Supreme Court nonetheless ordered him to release the tapes, and, mirabile dictu, Nixon complied. (Whether Donald Trump will comply in similar circumstances may yet be put to the test.)

These exceptions to judicial deference to the executive are, however, few and far between. It seems fair to predict that in the absence of more frequent and meaningful judicial review, presidents will be tempted to exceed their constitutional powers in order to realize their agendas. The Declaration of Independence is, in effect, a reaction to similarly excessive actions by King George III. With this example so clearly in mind, the Founding Fathers designed the Constitution in such a way that a wholly independent judiciary could, without fear or favor, enforce it, primarily against the legislature, but even against the president of the United States. It would be a tragedy if this constitutional design continued to be unrealized.

13

YOU WON'T GET YOUR DAY IN COURT

In prior chapters, I have described everything from the frequent and widespread failure of our criminal justice system to realize its proclaimed goals to the repeated failure of the Supreme Court to enforce the law of the land, especially against overreaching members of the executive branch. But there is a final and in some ways even more fundamental problem with our court system that must now be addressed. Over the past few decades, ordinary U.S. citizens have increasingly been denied effective access to their courts.

There are many reasons for this, including (1) the ever-greater cost of hiring a lawyer; (2) the increased expense, apart from legal fees, that a litigant must pay to pursue a lawsuit to conclusion; (3) the increased unwillingness of lawyers to take a case on a contingent-fee basis when the anticipated monetary award is modest; (4) the decline of unions and other institutions that provide their members with free legal representation; (5) the imposition of mandatory arbitration; (6) judicial hostility to class action suits; and (7) the increasing diversion of legal disputes to regulatory agencies. (In criminal cases, there is an eighth factor, already discussed in previous chapters, which is the vastly increased risk of a heavy penalty in going to trial.)

For these and other reasons, many Americans with ordinary legal disputes never get the day in court that they imagined they were guaranteed by the law. A further result is that most legal disputes are rarely decided by judges, and almost never by juries. And still another result is that the function of the judiciary as a check on the power of the executive and legislative branches and as an independent forum for the resolution of legal disputes has substantially diminished—with the all-too-willing acquiescence of the judiciary itself.

Some of this may seem surprising to people accustomed to hearing about overburdened courts with overcrowded dockets. These very real burdens partly reflect the decades-old refusal of many legislatures to provide funds for new courts and new judges at a rate remotely comparable to the increase in population and the corresponding increase in cases. But aside from these facts, a closer look at changes in the courts' dockets reveals some disturbing trends.

Until 1970, according to statistics compiled by the National Center for State Courts, the great majority of individuals who brought or defended lawsuits in state courts were represented by lawyers. But today as many as two-thirds of all individual civil litigants in state trial courts are representing themselves, without a lawyer. Indeed, in some states, an astonishing 90 percent of all family law and housing law cases—which are the most common legal disputes for most Americans—involve at least one party who is not represented by a lawyer.

Individuals not represented by lawyers lose cases at a considerably higher rate than similar individuals who are represented by counsel. In mortgage foreclosure cases, for example, you are twice as likely to lose your home if you are unrepresented by counsel. Or to give a different kind of example, if you are a survivor of domestic violence, your odds of obtaining a protective order fall by over 50 percent if you are without a lawyer. While hard statistics are not available for every kind of case, surveys of state and federal judges repeatedly show that they are quite certain that parties unrepresented by counsel fare far worse than those who are represented by counsel, even when the judge tries to compensate for counsel's absence.

This is hardly surprising. Unlike most European legal systems, where the judges play a more active role, the American legal system is an "adversary system," where, in Chief Justice John Roberts's words, the judge simply serves as an "umpire" determining which of the contestants has won the match. While the analogy may be overstated, the fact remains that very few laypersons, lacking a lawyer's legal education or familiarity with the intricacies of modern law, can hope to compete with a party represented by a lawyer. As a practical matter, such unrepresented litigants are effectively denied a fair day in court.

This is bad enough when the unrepresented litigant is a plaintiff who has chosen to go to court without a lawyer because she cannot afford one. But increasingly, the unrepresented parties are defendants who were hauled into court by institutions well supplied with lawyers. For example, the most immediate impact of the Great Recession on the courts was a huge increase in foreclosure proceedings brought by banks and other mortgage lenders against those who had defaulted on their mortgages. These hapless homeowners, who in many cases had been inveigled by mortgage brokers into taking out excessive mortgages on which they inevitably defaulted, were now facing foreclosure without remotely having the money to retain a lawyer to defend them.

Despite the subsequent improvement in the economy (prior to the COVID crisis), this peril persisted. In New York State, for example, almost one-third of all state court civil cases brought in 2015 were foreclosure actions; and in these, despite increased efforts by public interest groups to provide legal representation, nearly 40 percent of the defendants still were unrepresented. The same trend can also be seen in eviction proceedings brought against tenants. In New York City's Housing Court, for example, 70 percent of tenant defendants who were sued in 2015 were unrepresented by counsel.

More generally, most observers agree that the primary reason so many Americans are unrepresented in court is that even people of moderate means simply cannot afford a lawyer. The provision of legal services has never operated according to free-market principles. Lawyers comprise a guild to which there are significant barriers to entry, not least of which is the huge expense of a legal education. But in the past few decades, the price of hiring a lawyer to handle an everyday dispute has risen at a rate much greater than the average increase in income or wages. Thus, between 1985 and 2012, the average billing rate for law firm partners in the U.S. increased from $112 per hour to $536 per hour, and for associate lawyers from $79 per hour to $370 per hour. These billing rates increased at more than three times the rate of inflation during the same period.

Economists differ about the reasons for this large increase in the price of legal help. But among the causes is a great increase in legal specialization. A corollary is that the "family lawyer" has become even more rare than the "family doctor." But whereas the ordinary American can often get decent health care under insurance provided through his employer or, more recently, the state, affordable legal insurance remains a rarity. The result is not only that a very large number of Americans who go to court, or are hauled into court, are unrepresented by counsel, but also that an unknown but probably even larger number of Americans who might otherwise seek legal redress for wrongs done to them simply cannot afford a lawyer and choose instead to forgo justice altogether.

Further still, even those individuals who can afford counsel rarely get their day in court. Rather, in the overwhelming majority of cases, they settle with their adversaries before the merits of their cases ever get heard. This is true even in federal courts, where, because of lighter dockets, there is much less institutional pressure to settle. Nevertheless, whereas in 1938 about 19 percent of all federal civil cases went to trial, by 1962 that rate had declined to 11.5 percent and by 2015 it had declined to an abysmal 1.1 percent. Although the data for state civil cases are less ample, it appears that in state courts the situation is even worse, with fewer than 1 percent of state cases now going to trial. And while it is true that some of the remaining 99 percent of cases are resolved by pretrial motions, in the majority of cases the parties simply settle without any judge or jury reaching a decision on the merits.

To be fair, the pretrial settlement of a legal dispute is often a desirable result, and state court judges with their heavy dockets actively encourage settlement. But the fact that civil cases are being settled at an ever-greater rate suggests that something else is bringing pressure to settle, and it is probably the great expense of litigation. The United States, for example, allows pretrial discovery—that is, obtaining of documents, conducting of depositions, and the like—to a degree that far exceeds that of any other legal system in the world. While designed to achieve the laudable goal of preventing "trial by ambush," such broad discovery has proved to be excessively expensive. It thus not only places impecunious parties at a disadvantage but, again, also discourages ordinary people from bringing meritorious lawsuits in the first place.

A special case in point is certain kinds of common tort cases in which the American legal system has tried to mitigate the high cost of legal representation by allowing lawyers to enter into contingent-fee arrangements with their clients. Under these arrangements, the client does not pay the lawyer anything if the case is lost; but if it is won or settled, the lawyer gets to take a substantial percentage of the winnings or settlement fund as his or her fee.

The contingent-fee arrangement, however, has proved to be a limited cure, at best, for the problem of everyday Americans who cannot afford legal services. For one thing, contingent-fee arrangements only benefit those impecunious parties who are suing rather than being sued. Also, under the legal ethics rules of most jurisdictions, a plaintiff who brings a case on a contingent-fee basis is still personally responsible for paying for the costs of the lawsuit other than the attorney fees, and those costs frequently amount to thousands of dollars. Moreover, because the contingent-fee lawyer must hedge his bet by taking on a considerable number of cases, contingent-fee arrangements only operate in situations where the same kind of tort, such as a personal injury caused by a slip and fall on the sidewalk, recurs frequently and predictably. It also is widely believed, not just by defendants but also by many judges, that the contingent-fee arrangement encourages extortionate or even fabricated lawsuits. Most important, the time-consuming nature of modern litigation means that most contingent-fee lawyers will simply refuse to take on a case that does not promise an award or settlement of at least several hundred thousand dollars, leaving those tort victims who cannot sue for large amounts unable to have a day in court.

It also used to be that some people who could not afford a

lawyer had one provided for free by organizations to which they belonged, most commonly a union. But over the past few decades, the percentage of unionized workers in the private sector has steadily declined, and by 2015 it was down to 6.7 percent, a small fraction of the private workforce. So while the benefit of union-paid legal representation is still available to many government workers, it is largely unavailable to those in the private sector.

In addition to being priced out of legal services, many Americans, even those who can afford a lawyer's fee, are increasingly being forced to agree to one-sided contracts that prevent them from going to court altogether. For example, employees in an ever-growing percentage of the workforce must agree, as a condition of their employment, to contractual provisions that mandate that any legal disputes related to their employment be decided by a private arbitrator.

Similarly, consumers who purchase goods or services online are increasingly subject to terms and conditions unilaterally drafted by the sellers' lawyers that provide, among much else, that they must forgo their legal right to go to court, as well as their constitutional right to a jury, and instead have any and all disputes with the seller decided by a private arbitrator.

The private arbitrator not only is typically chosen and paid for by the employer or the seller but also is free to proceed with little or no regard for the ordinary rules of evidence and to decide the dispute without giving any reasons for the decision. The arbitrator is limited, however, in the relief she can afford employees or consumers even if she should find in their favor. So, for example, the company-imposed agreements that mandate arbitration typically also prohibit an award of punitive damages or the convening of a class action that would include others who have the same or similar complaints.

The latter is particularly significant, since the class action is one of the few devices that the American legal system has developed to offset the high cost of legal services. In particular, if numerous people suffer the same injury as a result of a company's misconduct, but no one person suffers an injury sufficiently large to offset the cost of hiring a lawyer, one or more of the injured parties can sue on behalf of the entire class of injured parties, making the case sufficiently lucrative for a lawyer to want to pursue it and making the outcome, if it is favorable to the plaintiff, sufficiently serious to have a deterrent effect on the company. But the class action suit—which most companies view with everything from skepticism to dread—is not available in a case before an arbitrator if the underlying agreement expressly prohibits class actions, as most such contracts increasingly do.

These agreements foisted on employees and consumers are what the law calls "contracts of adhesion," that is, one-sided contracts imposed on weaker parties who have no realistic ability to negotiate, let alone contest, the terms. But this has not deterred the courts, and especially the federal courts, from enforcing them.

Thus, for example, in 2011, the U.S. Supreme Court, in a 5–4 decision in the case of *AT&T Mobility LLC v. Concepcion*, effectively overruled the determination by the California Supreme Court that certain contracts of adhesion that mandated arbitration and prohibited class actions were unconscionable and unenforceable. The court held—in an opinion by Justice Antonin Scalia—that the California court's decision must give way to the supposed federal policy favoring the speed and efficiency of arbitration—as if, for example, the right to a jury trial guaranteed in federal civil cases by the Seventh Amendment (and in state civil cases by the constitutions of all but three states) were simply some outmoded procedure that could be forfeited in the interest of saving time.

The *Concepcion* case has attracted much criticism because of what some legal commentators view as its strained reasoning, which they typically ascribe to the pro-business slant of the Court's majority when Scalia was part of it. But its relevance here is to illustrate the lengths to which the courts themselves are prepared to go in restricting Americans' access to their own courts.

It is not just the courts that are to blame for limiting access to the courts. Congress, under both Democrats and Republicans, has enacted many kinds of laws restricting such access. An extreme example, discussed earlier, is the Antiterrorism and Effective Death Penalty Act, enacted with bipartisan support in 1996, which severely restricts the ability of a state prisoner to obtain the federal judicial review of his conviction that historically is embodied in the writ of habeas corpus. But a less-noticed example that actually affects many more average citizens is Congress's increasing delegation of judicial powers and responsibilities to administrative agencies. Without any obvious support from the Constitution, these agencies, though part of the executive branch of government, then create their own internal courts, with procedures that bear little resemblance to those found in ordinary courts. Furthermore, these administrative courts are run by judges who are selected by, paid by, and subject to review by the administrative agencies themselves.

Yet Congress, often at the behest of the president, has given increasing powers to these courts. For example, the Dodd-Frank Act of 2010 greatly expanded the powers of the Securities and Exchange Commission's administrative courts, including their power to impose severe monetary penalties on individuals. The SEC in turn has increasingly brought more of its important cases in its administrative courts, where, not surprisingly, its rate of success is considerably greater than its success rate in federal courts.

For its part, the Supreme Court has greatly limited its effective review of these administrative courts. In particular, the Court's 1984 decision in *Chevron USA v. Natural Resources Defense Council*, which severely limited the scope of judicial review of administrative regulations, has been extended to similarly limit judicial review of the decisions of administrative judges in any case in which the administrative agency has itself affirmed the decision of its administrative court, which it almost always does. The overall effect, once again, is to deprive ordinary people of meaningful access to regular courts.

While U.S. citizens thus no longer have much real access to their courts in many civil and regulatory matters, you might think they would still have meaningful access in criminal cases, which are beyond the jurisdiction of any administrative court, let alone private arbitrators. But as described in chapters 1 and 2, the real decisions in criminal cases are made by the prosecutors, not the courts. This is because, as a result of draconian and often mandatory penalties imposed by both Congress and most state legislatures during the last decades of the twentieth century, it is much too risky for any defendant, even an innocent one, to go to trial. Instead, over 97 percent of those charged in federal criminal cases negotiate plea bargains with the prosecution, and in the states collectively the figure is only slightly less, about 95 percent.

In most cases, as a practical matter (and sometimes as a legally binding matter as well), the terms of the plea bargain also determine the sentence to be imposed, so there is nothing left for either a judge or a jury to decide. While the immediate result is the so-called mass incarceration in the United States that has rightly become a source of shame for our country, the effect can also be seen as just one more example of the denial of meaningful access to the courts even in the dire circumstances of a criminal case.

Can anything be done about this increasing denial of access to the courts? A number of solutions have been proposed, ranging from state-sponsored legal insurance to a guarantee of counsel to indigent civil litigants to lawyer-subsidized provision of cheaper legal services for ordinary Americans. But none of these solutions would come easily. For example, Jonathan Lippman, the recently retired chief judge of New York State's highest court, has strongly advocated a right to counsel in civil cases similar to the right to counsel constitutionally guaranteed in criminal cases. But in New York, at least, this would require, according to Lippman, an amendment to the state constitution, a difficult change to bring about. And given the controversy over Obamacare, one can only imagine the difficulties that would attend any effort at the federal level to provide state-sponsored legal insurance. More generally, in view of the recurring gridlock in Congress and the history in state legislatures of short-changing legal aid groups, one cannot be very optimistic about any legislative solutions in the short run.

But while the broader solutions to this denial of access must await a change in the legislative climate, there is no reason for judges to continue to give their approval to devices that effectively deny Americans access to their courts. The Supreme Court, for example, could easily overrule or at least narrow decisions like *Concepcion* and *Chevron*, on the ground that they deprive Americans of meaningful access to their courts. And lower court judges, state and federal, could take a harder look at some of the practices described here that have the same effect.

Admittedly, this would require a considerable change of thought on the part of many judges. Indeed, it is hardly surprising that judges who often have substantial dockets tend to look favorably on arrangements that will lessen their work burden, whether by mandatory arbitration, denial of jurisdiction, reliance on prosecutors and administrators, or similar measures. Too often, however, such relief morphs into an effective abdication of judicial responsibility, with dire consequences for the long-term ability of the courts to serve as an effective check on the power of the legislature and the executive. Even worse, the situation I have described reinforces the belief of citizens that the courts are not an institution to which they can turn for justice, but simply a remote and expensive luxury reserved for the rich and powerful. If the judges themselves do not take steps to counter this insidious trend, who will?

CODA

The main object of this book has been to acquaint readers with the very substantial problems our judicial system currently faces. But it should be emphasized that virtually none of these problems are insolvable. At the same time, while judges should not shirk their responsibility to mitigate these problems (such as in ways I have suggested throughout this book), and certainly have a profound responsibility to bring these problems to the attention of the public, the most sweeping solutions must come from the legislatures. It is the legislatures, for example, that can repeal the shamefully harsh criminal laws they passed in the 1970s and 1980s, and thereby help reduce mass incarceration. It is the legislatures that can trim the powers of the executive branch in ways no court is likely to undertake. And it is the legislatures that can provide everyday people with meaningful access to their courts.

But, of course, the legislatures will not so act unless they are pushed in that direction by the voters. It was the voters who, for example, made it politically expedient for Congress to pass the

First Step Act, reducing mandatory minimum sentences, a step that would have been political suicide some twenty years earlier. Notwithstanding all the problems that attend the circulation of modern information, U.S. voters are not only among the most educated in the world but also among the most open to new ideas. So, even though I conclude that our legal system is in bad need of fixing, I remain cautiously optimistic that my fellow Americans will rise to the challenge.

ACKNOWLEDGMENTS

In late 2013, feeling an increasing need to speak out about the frailties of our legal system that I was witnessing in my court, I submitted, "cold," my first essay to *The New York Review of Books*. To my surprise and pleasure, I was immediately contacted by the co-founder and longtime editor of the *Review*, Bob Silvers (to whom this book is dedicated). Bob not only accepted my first effort for publication but also encouraged me to write further essays for the *Review*, which I have done ever since. After Bob's death in 2017, I received similar encouragement from his longtime deputy, Michael Shae, from his immediate successor, Ian Buruma, and from the current editors, Emily Greenhouse and Gabriel Winslow-Yost. They have my deepest thanks.

Each of the chapters in this book represents an expansion on essays that originally appeared in the *Review*. In their original form, they were edited and fact-checked by the utterly marvelous staff at the *Review*, to whom I owe a huge debt of gratitude. Any remaining errors are mine alone.

I have also been the beneficiary of the wonderful suggestions provided by the editors at Farrar, Straus and Giroux, including (but not limited to) Eric Chinski and Deborah Ghim, and by Janet Renard, who copyedited the manuscript. And at all stages I have received immense support from my literary agent, Chris Calhoun.

There are so many other people I should thank, such as my utterly brilliant and supportive law clerks; but for the sake of brevity I will finally mention the most important of all, my wife, Ann. Many were the evenings when I put off our going dancing (our hobby) in order to work on this book, and my sweet Ann never complained. But now that it's published, dear, I promise to practice all the best steps!

INDEX

A Note About the Author

Jed S. Rakoff is a senior judge of the United States District Court for the Southern District of New York and an adjunct professor at both Columbia University Law School and New York University Law School. Since going on the bench in 1996, Rakoff has authored more than 1,800 judicial opinions. He has served as a commissioner for the National Commission on Forensic Science and as cochair of the National Academy of Sciences' committee on eyewitness identification. He has also assisted the U.S. Departments of Commerce and State in training judges in a dozen countries. Rakoff is a regular contributor to *The New York Review of Books*. In 2014, he was listed by *Fortune* magazine as one of the World's 50 Greatest Leaders.